A Treasury of
Florida Tales

A Treasury of
Florida Tales

Webb Garrison

RUTLEDGE HILL PRESS
Nashville, Tennessee

Published in Nashville, Tennessee, by Rutledge Hill Press, Inc.
211 Seventh Avenue North, Nashville, Tennessee 37219.

Typography by Bailey Typography, Inc., Nashville, Tennessee

Library of Congress Cataloging-in-Publication Data

Garrison, Webb B.
    A treasury of Florida tales / Webb Garrison
      p.   cm.
    ISBN 1-55853-038 X
    1. Florida — History — Anecdotes. 2. Folklore — Florida.
I. Title.
F311.6.G37   1989   89-10610
975.9 — dc20   CIP

Published in the United States of America
3 4 5 6 7 8 — 98 97 96 95

Six Flags over Florida? Who's Kidding?

During nearly five hundred years, Florida has seen at least a dozen flags. All of the great European colonial powers—Spain, France, and England—saw "the land of flowers" as a place of national opportunity. As late as World War II, Nazi Germany eyed the peninsula for its own reasons.

Adventurers, would-be empire builders, and a utopian visionary shared one thing with Seminoles and other refugees. All of them were sure that Florida offered the haven they sought. Small wonder, therefore, that changes of government—sometimes local and often regional—took place more frequently here than in any other region of the United States.

Obviously, it is impossible in one thin volume to do more than paint a few broad strokes upon a vast canvas. Accepting this inevitable limitation, I have tried to depict a few of the diverse persons who made a lasting impact upon Florida or who used the state as a jumping-off place from which to affect the nation and the world.

This volume is in no sense a history of Florida.

Rather, it is a tribute to Floridians of many backgrounds and varied goals. All of the tales collected here are factual; "Florida's truth is stranger than the fiction of many regions." Letters, telegrams, diaries, and other documents are quoted rather freely, though usually greatly abbreviated from the originals. Dialogue has been collected from interviews, folklore, and oral tradition, amplified by

5

words true to situations and speakers, as heard by the inner ear.

All of this means that *A Treasury of Florida Tales* is both a book to enjoy and to share with others, as well as a source from which to get a better concept of the staggering scope of the Florida story. Therefore this book is addressed to Floridians by birth, Floridians by choice, those who would like to enhance memories of past visits, and others interested in preparing for future visits.

In addition to oral tradition, source material has come from numerous persons and institutions. At the top of the list is Secretary of State Jim Smith, whose agencies provided resources without which this volume could not have been prepared. Mary Ann Cleveland of the Florida State Library turned up not only conventional source material but also clippings and letters from obscure sources.

Others who provided great help include: Rachelle H. Saltzman, folk arts coordinator of the Bureau of Florida Folklife Programs; Soni Riddle of the Kissimmee-Saint Cloud Convention & Visitors Bureau; Kay Graham of the Henry Morrison Flagler Museum; Eileen M. Herrick, public affairs specialist at the U.S. Military Academy; Charlene W. Johnston of Bok Tower Gardens; Mrs. Bernice Dickson of the Hemingway Home and Museum; Lawrie Pitcher Platt of Tupperware Home Parties; Gertrude F. Laframboise of Rollins College Archives; and staff members at Fort Jefferson National Monument, the Stephen Foster Center, and the Gorrie Museum. To each, my heartfelt thanks,

—Webb Garrison

Contents

PART ONE

Three Centuries of Bloody Sand

For 325 years Florida was a nearly desolate prize that was fought over by the Spanish, the French, and the British—plus white-skinned, red-skinned, and black-skinned Americans.

Juan Ponce de León [Sixteenth-century Engraving]

1

Juan Ponce de León Was One of Spain's Most Splendid Failures

10 February 1521
Sire:
   Among my services, I have discovered, at my own expense, the Island of Florida and others in its district. I intend to explore the coast of the said island further, and see whether it connects with Cuba or any other; and I shall endeavor to learn all I can. I shall set out to pursue my voyage in five or six days.

Your faithful servant
De León

Writing to King Charles V of Spain, Juan Ponce de León did not anticipate that hostile Indians would attack his band of 250 men when they landed near today's Tampa Bay. However, they did. Seriously wounded, their leader retired to Cuba, where he died a few days later, regarding himself as a conspicuous failure.

Eight years earlier, at age 53, he had set out to find a marvelous fountain, or spring, whose potent waters would restore youth to those who drank them or bathed in them. Natives of Puerto Rico had told him of this great wonder, which he called Fons Juventutis or "fountain of youth."

The Spanish adventurer was determined to find the fountain and, for the glory of his king, to conquer the island of Bimini on which it was located. Convinced that trees around the fountain bore "fruit of gold" that beautiful maidens plucked and presented to strangers, with three caravels he set out to master Bimini and its wonders.

On March 27, 1513, Ponce de León sighted land, which he called in Spanish *Florida*, meaning "feast of flowers," a term linked with Easter. In a brief but formal ceremony on what he believed to be a big island, he took possession of it in the name of Spain.

Nowhere in Florida did he come close to reaching his goal, the miraculous fountain. Neither did he succeed in his secondary, but still vital, purpose of discovering gold in abundance. Early European drawings depicted Indians of the country north of present-day Jacksonville retrieving gold from a river. Although he probably passed through that region, Ponce de León found no yellow metal.

Thus eight years and many adventures after having found, named, and claimed Florida for his sovereign, de León regarded himself as a failure.

He was sure there were wonders aplenty in the region. He had been told that native rulers were giants because as children their bones had been treated with herbs that made them stretch. He looked for, but never saw, such giants.

His search for "men with tails, which they could lash fearsomely about," was equally futile. Even lions and kangaroos, which natives told him were abundant, eluded the Spanish adventurer.

In a region where his men killed 170 tortoises in a single day, he did manage to map a cluster of tiny islands that he called the Tortugas, or Turtles. And he recorded in his diary with wonder a notation about the location of an immense river that flowed through the ocean day and night without ceasing. That, plus his huge island—minus gold and a marvelous fountain—was all he had to show for his years of hardship and danger.

De León's followers thought more highly of him than he did of himself. When he was formally buried, on his tomb was inscribed, "In this Sepulchre rest the Bones of a Man who was Leon (lion) by Name, and still more by Nature."

It was decades before anyone in Europe realized that

"Terra Florida," Cuba, and South America as depicted in 1540 (land areas are white). [PTOLEMY'S GEOGRAPHY]

Ponce de León's "immense island" was actually a peninsula 400 miles long. Once the true nature of Florida was realized, Spain claimed all North America as her own. For more than a century, Florida was used to name the region from the Gulf of Mexico to the Appalachian Mountains, as well as unknown and unexplored Indian country beyond the mountains.

Long afterward, the thirty-mile-per-hour "great river in the ocean" that Ponce de León found was named the Gulf Stream, one of the globe's most important features. Coupled with what he died believing to be a big island, the Gulf Stream places the man who found neither fountain nor gold among the front rank of all-time great discoverers.

St. Augustine is a "living monument" to Ponce de León and the oldest city in what is now the United States. To savor St. Augustine and its wonders, visitors should plan to spend two or three days there. Details about it are available from the Visitor Information Center at 10 Castillo Drive, telephone (904) 824-3334.

2

Ten Squadrons of Frenchmen Marched Across Dunes to Death

"Are you Catholics or Lutherans, and are there any who wish to confess the Catholic faith?"

Shouted by a Spanish officer to wounded, hungry, and absolutely weary French captives on a September day in 1565, the question was ignored by many. A few especially bold young officers shook their heads and shouted defiance.

Admiral Pedro Menéndez de Avilés gave a pre-arranged signal. In response, a subordinate directed thirty captives to separate themselves from their comrades. At his instructions, the little company marched over the sand dunes, out of sight and hearing.

Soon, though, another company of men was sent in the same direction. Then another, and another, until three hundred had left the improvised compound in which they were imprisoned.

Spanish officers knew then, and the world learned later, that each company of Frenchmen halted upon command. Then Spanish soldiers shot them in cold blood. Upon the ruins of the French fort he had captured, Menéndez erected a crude cross bearing the legend, "Not as to Frenchmen, but as Lutherans."

Menéndez had reached the site of St. Augustine on September 8, bearing specific orders from King Philip II of Spain: "You are to find out whether there are on the coast or country of Florida any settlers who are corsairs, or of any nations not subject to us." Should such intruders upon Spain's North American dominion be found, the job of the special force was to "cast them out by the best means that seems to you possible."

With a force that may have numbered 2,500, Menéndez had hardly beached his vessels at St. Augustine before he discovered that he would have to act decisively. French Huguenots had established Fort Caroline on the St. Johns River. Clearly, they expected to make it a permanent haven for persecuted Protestants of France.

Headed by Jean Ribault, who had made at least one earlier voyage to Florida, the French settlement was large and prosperous. It threatened Spain's territorial aims; worse, it would soon become a troublesome boil upon the body of the one true church.

Ribault, a veteran seaman with several fast vessels at his command, welcomed an opportunity to fight at sea. But he failed to take into account the then-unfamiliar weather phenomenon known today as the hurricane. Three of Ribault's ships went to the bottom during a great tempest; with six hundred men, he reached shore and prepared to fight on land.

Overwhelmingly superior Spanish forces swarmed over Fort Caroline on the morning of September 20 and killed 132 Frenchmen without losing a man themselves. That left Ribault and his forces stranded on a beach. When they

Pedro Mendéndez de Avilés [SEVENTEENTH-CENTURY ENGRAVING]

surrendered on October 10, all of them refused to give up their faith and were marched over the dunes to their death.

In Paris news of the New World massacre enraged Dominic de Gourges. With a picked company of veterans, he sailed for Florida and launched a surprise attack upon the Spanish-held fort on the St. Johns River. The French victory was followed by a mass hanging of the Spanish garrison. Near their dangling bodies a new cross was erected with the message, "Not as to Spaniards, but as murderers." Not having enough men to attack St. Augustine, however, Gourges returned home, ending the French bid to colonize Florida.

Several other bold and colorful Spanish leaders had appeared during the interval between Ponce de León and Menéndez. Hernando De Soto, the best known of them, wandered through much of the southeast in search of gold. At his death, his men dropped his body into the Mississippi River to prevent its falling into the hands of hostile Indians.

Francisco de Garay, also seeking gold without success, claimed to have found native American tribes whose chiefs were giants and whose warriors were pigmies. Pánfilo de Narváez led a band north of the Suwannee River,

Fort Caroline, as imaginatively depicted by a European artist in 1671. [Seventeenth-century Engraving]

Followers of Hernando De Soto buried him in the Mississippi River.

where Indians are said to have captured and enslaved them.

Keenly aware of these and other disastrous expeditions, Menéndez wisely stayed close to the sea. His base, St. Augustine, grew in size and strength. Spanish missionaries who converged upon it fanned out and established at least twenty missions. Today, a 208-foot stainless steel cross marks the site at which Menéndez—ruthless killer of French Protestants—established the first permanent European city in North America.

Yet the hapless French are not forgotten. In 1742, the Spanish used coquina, a construction material made of shell and coral fragments, to build a fort at the site of the sixteenth-century massacre. They called it *matanzas*, or "slaughters."

Today, Fort Matanzas National Monument includes parts of both Anastasia and Rattlesnake islands. Situated about fourteen miles south of St. Augustine, it may be reached by ferry. The monument provides a unique glimpse into the dimly remembered past when Spain, France, and England each hoped and expected to hold Florida forever. Allow at least two hours for a visit to the Anastasia Island site of the monument.

3

Invasion — "For the Glory of England and the Security of Georgia"

"His Majesty clearly means much more than he writes," mused Gen. James Oglethorpe. Georgia's founder and trustee in residence spoke largely to himself. But Mary Musgrove, the Yamacraw "princess" who was his interpreter and Indian agent, acted as though she knew precisely what he meant.

"Listen again," directed her employer. "His Majesty, writing on June 15, orders me 'to annoy the Subjects of Spain, and to put the Colonies of Carolina and Georgia in the best posture of Defence.'"

Oglethorpe paced silently for a period, then turned to Mary Musgrove and said, "Ride to your people at once! Tell them that I need every able-bodied warrior. We are going to beard the Spanish lion in his own den—St. Augustine!"

On September 9, 1739, a historic pact was drawn up and accepted promising the Cherokees a substantial shipment of grain. In return, they pledged to provide six hundred of their finest fighting men for the upcoming invasion of Florida. Simultaneously, Oglethorpe issued a call for help from Cherokees and a plea for every available man from the "home guard" of his nearest English neighbor to the north, the Carolina Colony.

However, although leaders in Charles Town were keenly aware that the Spanish had occupied nearby Port Royal, they vacillated at the "imperious ways" of James Oglethorpe from Georgia, the youngest and weakest of Britain's North American colonies. Compared with

General James Edward
Oglethorpe, M. P.

strongly fortified Charles Town, Savannah was at best a
frontier stockade.

While Carolina debated and wavered, Oglethorpe acted.
With a small force he made a quick raid into Florida and
captured two small outposts of little strategic importance.
This was hailed as a great victory, proving that the Spanish were not invincible. Encouraged, Oglethorpe set to
work erecting for himself an advance post about twenty-
five miles northeast of present-day Jacksonville.

Eventually Carolina provided a fraction of the men and
money originally requested. The soldiers were placed at
Oglethorpe's disposal so late that his original timetable
for the campaign against St. Augustine could not be followed. This delay permitted reinforcement by Spanish
forces from Cuba and made weather a major factor.

To add to Oglethorpe's difficulties, his Indian allies,
who had been eager to accept his gifts, failed him now.
Instead of two thousand native American warriors, his invasion army included only about two hundred. Since
one-third of his regiment was needed for garrison duty in
Georgia, Oglethorpe had less than four hundred regulars
with which to attack seasoned Spanish veterans. Colonial
rangers and short-time recruits from Carolina reported in
small numbers.

Commanders of British warships in southern waters
had received special messages from King George II. He
reminded them that with no land force to support the
crew of his ship, Sir Francis Drake had taken the offensive
against St. Augustine in 1586. Swarming over the town in

a surprise attack, English fighting men had conquered the Spanish fort, which they had leveled when they burned the town it defended. Twenty years later, buccaneers under Capt. John Davis had again pillaged St. Augustine and had again—briefly—seen the British flag fly over the strategic site.

"England's honor is again at stake," the British monarch informed the men of the Royal Navy in American waters. "You are to heed the instructions of Gen. James Oglethorpe in every particular."

In spite of specific orders from their king, the British captains gave priority to the approaching hurricane season. By the time Oglethorpe was ready to march toward Florida, nearly all of the vessels upon which he had counted for support had left for safer southern waters.

Long delays were matched by slow movement of troops. Tiny Fort Mosa, a Spanish outpost far north of St. Augustine, was captured by the English, then recaptured by the Spanish. English fighting men and their Indian allies wasted much precious time and energy in futile marches designed to demonstrate their strength and to frighten the Spanish into easy submission.

Not until June, 1740, were British forces encamped around St. Augustine. A larger and much stronger fortress, or "Castillo," had been built on the ruins of the one destroyed by Drake and his men. Clearly, concluded James Oglethorpe, it was too powerful to be the target of a frontal assault. So he would besiege the fortress, and the town.

Oglethorpe's men were sure they were fighting for the glory of England and the security of Georgia. They managed to effect a strong siege line that cut St. Augustine off from the rest of Florida; but, lacking effective sea power with which to throw up a blockade of the port, Oglethorpe saw it daily supplied by Spanish vessels.

After three weeks, the oldest European settlement on the continent showed no signs of weakening. Food and water remained in good supply, and only a few Spanish soldiers had fallen in combat.

Meanwhile, however, malaria had invaded the camps of

St. Augustine's public square as it appeared when the city was about two hundred years old.

the besiegers. Since on July 5 the remaining British vessels in the region would set sail to avoid the approaching hurricane season, on July 4 Oglethorpe burned much of the town, then ordered the siege of St. Augustine abandoned.

Judged by any standard, the British foray into Spanish Florida was a debacle. The invaders had not succeeded in provoking a significant military engagement, and General Oglethorpe was clearly bested. Many Carolina leaders, who had hesitated to lend their support to the invasion, were furious at its outcome. They made it clear that no more help of any kind could be expected from the wealthy old colony.

Manuel de Montiano, governor of Florida, spoke for many European observers when he said of the invasion by the British, "I cannot arrive at a comprehension of the conduct, or rules of this British general."

James Oglethorpe's planned "mighty blow" was delivered with so little effect that it could only be compared with a futile swat at a mosquito. Spain remained in firm control of Florida, a region that its sovereigns continued to insist stretched indefinitely to the north and all the way to the Mississippi River in the west.

Those who deceived themselves could continue to call Florida "the debatable land," but the subtropical portion of North America remained firmly in Spanish control.

4

A Fair Swap: All Florida for Havana and West Cuba

"England will wrest North America from France and Spain," an impassioned William Pitt promised members of Parliament. He did not mention James Oglethorpe's aborted invasion of Florida a generation earlier. Although Florida—and all of North America—was involved, the decisive military engagements would take place in Europe.

During the Seven Years' War of 1756-63, the struggle between the European powers became global. Germany was the crucial spot, but French soldiers battled English soldiers in India as well as in Canada. Drawn into the struggle between the great powers, natives of Senegal were forced to take sides in the conflict that in America was called the French and Indian War.

Warships of His Majesty's Navy converged upon Havana, the richest Spanish prize north of the equator in the Americas, and forced quick surrender. Gen. James Wolfe led British and Colonial troops against Quebec, where he defeated the great French strategist, the Marquis de Montcalm. In Germany, England furnished much of the money needed by Frederick the Great, whose victories influenced the future of Europe.

Under the terms of the 1763 Treaty of Paris, there were no significant changes in European borders. However, France had to abandon India, relinquish to Britain all its territory on the North American mainland east of the Mississippi, and cede to Spain all her American holdings west of the Mississippi and at its mouth. France thereby

William Pitt promised that England would take Florida from France and Spain.

abandoned the North American continent. Clearly, England was marked as the emerging superpower of the era.

Although Britain had taken Havana in 1762, she returned it to Spain in exchange for Spain's Florida possessions, thereby consolidating British American holdings down the eastern seaboard and to the Mississippi.

They then divided Florida into East Florida, with St. Augustine as capital, and West Florida, with Pensacola as capital.

Soon Florida's new owners pushed the northern boundary of West Florida northward to include much of present-day Louisiana, Mississippi, and Alabama. Both Floridas were formally converted into royal colonies, for which London provided generous financial support.

At this time, St. Augustine had almost four thousand inhabitants, including 315 black slaves, 95 free blacks, and 89 Indians who had adopted the Catholic faith. Pensacola, the new capital in the west, was only one-fourth as large.

When news of the transfer reached the New World, Spanish citizens packed up their possessions and left in a hurry. Their departure made England's new American possessions virtually uninhabited, except for roving bands of Indians.

James Grant and George Johnstone were named royal

governors of East Florida and West Florida, respectively. Johnstone could do little more than try to strengthen the already formidable military installations in Pensacola.

But it was a different story in East Florida. It was a prize that some considered to be worth plucking. Dr. Andrew Turnbull procured a grant of land in 1767, and immediately started to recruit settlers in a more methodical fashion than that employed earlier by John White.

Turnbull focused his attention upon poverty-stricken peasants of the Mediterranean basin. During a period of two years, he induced at least two thousand Italians, Minorcans, and Greeks to come to Florida. He provided land and tried to teach them to raise rice, sugar, indigo, and maize, the versatile cereal that Americans today call corn.

Matters seemed to be progressing well in East Florida until truculent colonists to the north launched what they termed "a revolution against British tyranny." Spain pretended to take a neutral stance, but in actuality it did everything possible to aid rebellious colonies, hoping to weaken England.

In Britain's original thirteen North American colonies, patriots stripped Loyalists of their possessions. Many of those refugees flocked to East Florida, causing the prewar population of 5,000 to grow by 5,000 white Loyalists and 8,300 slaves in a single year, 1783.

George Washington and his patriots stunned the world by their victories, which set the stage for new rounds of diplomacy in preparation for another peace treaty. Benjamin Franklin, John Adams, and John Jay represented the new nation at the Paris parleys that brought the American Revolution to a formal end.

Under terms of the 1783 Treaty of Versailles, independence of the United States of America was recognized. Americans promised, in turn, to cease their persecution of Loyalists. To indemnify Spain for her war expenditures, the British returned Florida to the empire ruled by King Charles III.

Britain had held Florida for twenty years, and the American Loyalists who had gone there were dismayed

In Paris, Benjamin Franklin assented to Spain's proposal that England give her Havana in exchange for Florida.

when they learned the terms of the treaty. Unwilling to remain as subjects of Catholic Spain, at least 13,000 persons, including many of the colonists brought over by Dr. Turnbull, fled to the Caribbean islands or Nova Scotia, considered to be firmly in British hands.

Living in retirement on his Irish estates in County Down, the Earl of Hillsborough bemoaned the loss of the region he had long called his "favorite colony." He had spent just enough time in Florida to realize that it was distinctly different from the colonies to the north, but no one in a position of authority listened when the aging nobleman pleaded for England to "recover her crown jewel, Florida, from Spain before it is too late."

Spanish leaders showed no signs of regret at the hasty exodus that followed the change of ownership. Neither did they take seriously the small but rapidly increasing stream of American emigrants who had begun to move into Florida from the north. With France out of mainland America and England now confined to Canada, what possible danger could stem from a fledgling United States of America that had little interest in East and West Florida, except a common border?

5

Haven for Runaways and Renegades Was Hellhole for Prisoners

"Who brought this letter of which so much has been said, and who was its writer?" demanded Gen. Charles Lee, second in command to Gen. George Washington.

At Lee's command post in Charles Town, Carolina Colony, aides responded promptly. "A gentleman from Georgia brought the letter on Tuesday," one of them explained. "It was found along the trail that links this city with St. Augustine.

"As to the writer," he continued, "the signature page is missing. But those who know him are certain that it comes from the hand of Thomas Heyward."

A native of St. Luke's Parish in Carolina, Heyward had served on the Council of Safety and in the Continental Congress. Presently he was known to be confined in the huge stone castillo (prison) at St. Augustine, along with two other signers of the Declaration of Independence and a group of about sixty other notable citizens of Carolina.

"Florida has long been known as a haven for refugees and renegades," said the letter brought from Georgia. "Everyone knows that the place is good for nothing else. But now that the Redcoats have put it to use as a place of imprisonment, it is suddenly valuable to them.

"Here a runaway, whether he be white or red or black, can find safety," continued the document believed to have been written by Heyward. "And here a prisoner has no hope of rescue. It is a hellhole of pestilence and fever, useful to the British precisely because it punishes while

General Charles Lee [SOUTH CAROLINA STATE LIBRARY]

providing absolute security from the help of fellow patriots."

Lee, a native of Cheshire in England who had entered the army as a child and had won a commission at age eleven, was both incensed and challenged. He had fought for England's glory in Canada and for his own advancement in Poland. Now he was siding with the rebellious American colonists and had accepted the rank of major general after Congress had guaranteed him $30,000 in indemnity for loss of estates confiscated in England.

Impulsive, sharp-tongued, and egotistical, Lee had spent time among the Mohawk Indians. When he was adopted into a tribe, chieftains gave him a name that in their language meant "boiling water."

At Charles Town in 1780, Boiling Water saw a glorious opportunity in Florida. Without consulting people who were familiar with the region, he announced that he would personally lead a raiding party to St. Augustine.

He would liberate Edward Rutledge, Arthur Middleton, Thomas Heyward, and perhaps half a hundred other patriots from their hellhole of a prison. That would elevate Lee to the front rank of heroes among men fighting the British, and it would atone for humiliation suffered when Charles Town was attacked by the Spanish in 1706.

Hasty inquiry had convinced Lee that Florida was, indeed, a refuge for renegades, and had been so for generations. Since 1670, when Charles Town was founded, slaves had periodically tried to escape to Florida. Those who reached the peninsula and who professed the Catholic faith were accepted and given small tracts of land. So many of them reached this haven that the Spanish created from them special militia units, stationed chiefly at Fort Mosa. In time this outpost became generally known as the "Negro Fort."

A community of civilians grew up around the "Negro Fort," populated by Africans, Indians, *mulattos* (combination of Negro-white blood), *mestizos* (combination of Indian-white blood), and the racial group that the Spanish called *zambos* (combination of Negro-Indian blood).

Yuchee Indians of Georgia often sent raiding parties into the region north of St. Augustine. They seized runaway slaves but also captured Christian Indians and a few of their Spanish masters. Such persons were taken to Charles Town and sold as slaves.

About the time that Gen. James Oglethorpe made his futile invasion of Florida, the region was swarming with blacks from South Carolina. Natives of Angolo, situated chiefly on plantations along the Stono River, had revolted and had managed to secure arms. They had killed twenty-three whites before companies of militia drove them into the swamps where about forty were killed and the rest were scattered. Those survivors of the revolt whose injuries permitted rapid travel through forests and swamps found safety in Florida, where the Spanish governor issued an unconditional promise of freedom.

Once the British, long eager to oust the Spanish, gained possession of Florida, Gov. James Grant circulated immigration invitations. When the outbreak of the American Revolution brought a flood of new settlers, so many came that there was not enough cultivated land to feed them. One such newcomer was the celebrated Tory, Rory McIntosh. A letter of the time describes him as strutting the streets of St. Augustine on "public days." Wearing full Highland costume and attended by a piper, Rory was described as about sixty-five years of age, six feet in height, strongly built, with white bushy hair and large whiskers "frizzled fiercely out." As a local celebrity, his presence in Florida was particularly vexatious to patriots.

To make the Florida situation worse, Tory refugees formed alliances with Creek Indians and from time to time made predatory raids beyond the St. Marys River. Gen. Robert Howe tried to retaliate in 1778, but his expedition managed to go only a short distance south of the Ogeechee River.

All of these factors seem to have influenced the decision of General Lee to march upon St. Augustine, with little preparation and less planning. During the second week of August 1780, their commander dispatched troops of Virginia and North Carolina. Gen. William Moultrie, who had distinguished himself by defending Charles Town from British warships, was also ordered to take his men south.

Most Continental soldiers who were headed for St. Augustine made the trip from Charles Town to Savannah by water. They managed to take along two light field pieces and a quantity of ammunition for their rifles. Encamped and waiting for new orders from their commander, the patriots were hit by fever. Casualties mounted so rapidly that soon "fourteen or fifteen men were buried daily."

Reluctant to move toward his objective so long as fever raged among his troops, Lee dallied so long that in September he received orders to proceed north to join General Washington. General Moultrie, placed in charge of troops still quartered in Georgia, promptly called off the Florida campaign. Tradition says that he declared "the pest-hole called St. Augustine is not worth the life of a single brave American."

Edward Rutledge and many of his imprisoned comrades were exchanged in 1781, but Florida's reputation as a hellhole for prisoners was revived nearly a century later, when some of the nation's most celebrated prisoners were sent to Fort Jefferson, on the Dry Tortugas Islands.

Long after fever thwarted the ambitions of Gen. Charles Lee, Florida continued to be a haven for outlaws and runaways. A colony of blacks and Indians, led by an ex-slave named Garcia, took possession of an abandoned British fort after the War of 1812.

Their installation resisted all challenges by authorities until 1816, when Col. Duncan L. Clinch led U.S. Army troops against it. Garcia and a Choctaw chief who served as his aide were killed when the powder magazine exploded. Of 350 persons in the fortress, only about 50 survived the mighty blast. Verbal reports of the time insisted that from the outlaw stronghold on the Apalachicola River, soldiers retrieved stolen property valued at $200,000.

South American soldier of fortune Gregor MacGregor chose Florida as the site for a planned military move against Spain. His mercenaries were quartered briefly at Fernandina, which he seized in the name of Simón Bolívar. When MacGregor pulled out, his empty base was briefly occupied by soldiers led by Luis Aury, who claimed the region in the name of the Republic of Mexico. A U.S. naval operation drove the Mexicans out in 1817 and claimed Amelia Island as American soil.

Meanwhile, more and more "runaways" from the Creek nation—calling themselves Seminoles—settled in the swamps of Florida. Both Spanish and English authorities generally ignored the Seminoles, who were difficult or impossible to capture and were not numerous enough to present a threat. So it seemed in the first decade of the nineteenth century.

While the Seminoles were filtering into East Florida in increasing numbers, leaders in faraway Washington City eyed the region with renewed interest. Many held that it should belong to the United States of America, not Spain, France, or England.

Encouragement, and perhaps some money, flowed from Washington to Georgia, when George Mathews, a former governor of Georgia, led an expedition into Florida hoping to overthrow the Spanish government. Fernandina, on Amelia Island, was the base of his operation that lasted nearly a year.

Congress apparently authorized the Mathews expedition in a secret session. At the same time, American lawmakers encouraged the president of the United States "to seize West Florida, if a foreign power attempts to take possession."

Mathews was barely out of the region before John H. McIntosh led a band of settlers to the northern border of Florida. There he announced the formation of a new nation: the Republic of East Florida.

With McIntosh as president and Colonel Ashley as commander-in-chief of armed forces of the republic, Americans moved upon Fernandina. They captured the fort and ousted the Spanish garrison, then headed for St. Augustine. Protests from Madrid led Washington to disavow any connection with the republic. Without support from the north, East Florida's new government collapsed and its leaders fled or were imprisoned.

Visitors to Fort George Island may still see one of the few tangible reminders of Florida's most checkered era. At the Kingsley Plantation State Historic Site, the 1792 residence briefly occupied by the president of the Republic of East Florida may be toured, Thursdays through Mondays. For more information about the historic site, call (904) 251-3122.

6

Bernardo de Gálvez Acted Without Instructions

"War!" exclaimed an aide to youthful Bernardo de Gálvez, Spanish governor of Louisiana. "It has finally come; the British Parliament took action six weeks ago—on June 21."

In 1779 Spanish leaders in the New World waited expectantly for precisely the events that took place. Once England had declared war upon Spain, Spain redoubled her efforts to aid rebellious American colonists in their struggle against their mother country. But King Charles III of Spain, accused by courtiers of being so cautious that he seemed cowardly, was in no hurry to confront his long-standing enemy on the seas. The British Royal Navy claimed to rule the waves. Hence Charles refused to endorse plans for immediate, direct military action, a course that frustrated his colonial governors.

In New Orleans Gálvez weighed the challenges and risks. Should he fail in an unauthorized strike against the British, he could rely upon help at the court from his father and uncle. One was a viceroy in South America, the other a minister of the Indies.

Having made friends with many bands of Creek Indians and having recruited Alexander McGillivray as an aide, Gálvez decided not to wait for orders from Madrid. According to his spies, the British in West Florida—bounded on the east by the Apalachicola River—had not yet received war news. Very well. He would strike before they heard it and had time to prepare.

With a mixed body of Spanish veterans and Indian allies, Gálvez marched into Natchez and ousted the British

Bernardo de Gálvez and his men before Fort George.

authorities there without firing a shot. Then he swiftly took possession of all other British settlements on the east bank of the Mississippi River.

By the time he returned to his New Orleans base, a message was waiting for him. According to the captain-general of Cuba—his immediate superior—it would be unwise to take additional military action.

"He cautioned me, but he did not forbid me to proceed," reasoned the young nobleman. "That means he is being careful not to offend our sovereign. But it also means he may be willing to come to my aid, if necessary. I will settle for nothing less than West Florida in its entirety."

By January 1780, Gálvez had assembled 11 ships and at least 745 men. He believed they would be more than enough to move against Mobile.

North winds blowing through the Gulf of Mexico impeded his progress, so it was the middle of February before his men began to erect positions from which to besiege Mobile. Days later, 567 Spanish veterans arrived to bolster his force. The captain-general of Cuba had, indeed, seen the necessity for striking before receiving orders from Madrid!

Redcoats in the miniature fortress, about three hundred in number, swore they would hold out indefinitely. But they watched appalled as reinforcements came ashore. When the overwhelmingly superior Spanish force breached the wall in two places, the British capitulated.

Their surrender left just one major British outpost in West Florida: Pensacola, a permanent settlement since the Spanish built Fort San Carlos there in 1698. Almost entirely dependent upon food shipped from a distance, the city had been defeated in 1719 when French naval vessels threw up a tight blockade. Returned to Spain in 1723 and then involved in the Florida/Cuba exchange, Pensacola had been enlarged and strengthened by successive governments. During nine changes of ownership, it became one of the strongest citadels in North America.

Sir Henry Clinton, who commanded all British forces in North America, went to great lengths to place Georgia under his control, but he showed no interest at all in Flor-

Sir Henry Clinton, British commander-in-chief in the New World, failed to recognize the strategic importance of Pensacola.

ida. Perhaps he failed to realize that Canada on the north and Florida on the south could serve as staging points from which to put thirteen rebellious colonies between the jaws of a vise.

By the time Spain declared war upon England in 1779, Gálvez had perfected his plan to strip the island kingdom of one of her North American colonies. It took him more than a year to assemble sixty-four ships and four thousand men at Havana. With his mighty flotilla, the Spanish governor entered Pensacola Bay on March 8, 1781.

Inside the fortress that the British had renamed Fort George in honor of their own sovereign, the commander doubted that a frontal assault would succeed, but he was keenly aware of his inability to withstand a prolonged siege. He and his men held out bravely for more than two weeks. When they watched the debarkation of an additional one thousand Spanish troops in late March, they began conversations with Gálvez and his generals.

Pensacola surrendered on May 9, 1781.

Few present-day Americans have ever heard of the siege and battle of Pensacola, but some historians rank it as perhaps the most important engagement of the Revolutionary era. England continued to hold Canada and East Florida, but the loss of her sixteenth North American colony, which commanded much of the Gulf of Mexico, meant that she forfeited her opportunity to attack the American rebels from the north and south.

With Pensacola fallen and all West Florida in Spanish hands, King George III agreed that, after just twenty years of British administration, the remainder of Florida should be returned to the Spanish.

What if? is a question that can seldom be answered accurately, and yet it must sometimes be posed. What if British leaders had strengthened Pensacola sufficiently to withstand a prolonged siege and blockade?

There are no firm answers to this question, but it is within the realm of possibility that had Pensacola—and West Florida—been retained, the entire southeastern tip of North America might still be British.

7

"The French, Spanish, and Seminoles Must Go — Now"

Elected to the presidency at a time when Americans were trying to enforce an embargo upon British and French goods, James Madison had hardly taken office before he was publicly denounced. Stalwarts of his own Republican party called him "unfit to fill the office of President in the present juncture of our affairs."

It was in this context that, recognizing that England or France (or both) might use military force at any time and that public sentiment called for strong measures, Madison decided to take action. He seized upon Florida as an issue behind which he hoped to unite the divided nation. After a long series of secret meetings with congressional leaders and with members of his cabinet, Madison called for immediate U.S. ownership of all Florida. A newspaper summed up his views in a single brief sentence: "The French, the Spanish, and the Seminoles must go—now!"

All Florida west of Alabama's Perdido River belonged to France by virtue of a 1795 deal with Spain, but Thomas Jefferson had purchased Louisiana from France. Boundaries of the territory were not clearly specified; in the West, they were not even known. So Madison seized upon the agreement with France as an excuse to claim that the United States had secured title to West Florida by means of the Louisiana Purchase.

West Florida authorities found themselves all but helpless. Numerous Americans had moved into the region, and they had no intention of respecting the sovereignty of

38

Gen. Andrew Jackson—"Old Hickory"

France, regardless of what a court of international law might say.

Madison's 1810 decision to move immediately to rid Florida of the French, Spanish, and Seminoles was welcomed by Americans who had settled in the contested region. Probably (but not positively) with covert aid and encouragement from Washington, a band of insurgents seized the fort at Baton Rouge late in the year. They held a convention, declared their part of West Florida to be an independent republic, and claimed all unallocated land in the French colony. Hastily recruited bands of soldiers marched behind a flag bearing a single star and presented their demands to the governor of the Mississippi Territory. They wanted a loan of one hundred thousand dollars and blanket pardon for all deserters from the U.S. Army.

Forwarded to President Madison, these demands gave him the opportunity he had been seeking. He issued a proclamation claiming the entire east bank of the Mississippi River as part of the United States. At Mobile, not yet transferred to France by the Spanish, Governor Juan Vicente Folch hinted that he was willing to negotiate for the transfer of all West Florida to the United States.

Congress responded by passing an act authorizing the president "to take immediate possession of both West Florida and East Florida, in order to prevent these provinces from falling into the hands of an enemy."

At about the same time that insurgents created their one-star republic in West Florida, Gen. James Matthews of the Georgia militia was named president of the Republic of East Florida. Unlike fellow adventurers in the west, Matthews was supported by a small body of U.S. soldiers.

By this time, war with Great Britain had become a reality. A British fleet sailed into Pensacola harbor, and soldiers of His Majesty King George III took possession of Forts Michel and Barrancas in August 1814.

With the full support of the president, Gen. Andrew Jackson led five thousand Tennessee volunteers into French/Spanish territory. They captured Pensacola on November 7, 1814, effectively gained possession of West Florida, and immediately began making plans to move upon East Florida. There the Spanish maintained nominal authority, but the Seminoles presented the only real threat to American seizure.

Andrew Jackson and his troops made foray after foray into East Florida, strongly supported by Creeks whom Jackson had earlier crushed in battle. The Seminoles were getting help from some European source, Jackson reasoned. If not guns and ammunition, certainly they were

Because of the Arbuthnot and Ambrister affair, political foes depicted Jackson as a hangman.

receiving encouragement and leadership, probably from Spanish authorities.

Old Hickory, as Jackson was called by his soldiers, moved into Florida once more in April 1818. He was astonished to discover among a band of captured Seminoles a Scottish trader, Alexander Arbuthnot. Perhaps native warriors who preyed upon Americans were being aided by America's old enemies, the British!

A small coastal vessel under Jackson's command was ordered to hoist the British flag. Within hours, two Indian chieftains took refuge upon it.

Andrew Jackson ordered the renegades to be hanged without trial, then marched against a Seminole town on the Suwannee River. He captured and burned it, discovering that Indians and runaway slaves who defended it were led by another British subject, Robert Ambrister.

Hauled before a court-martial, Arbuthnot and Ambrister were convicted of "having stirred up the Indians to war." Both were British subjects, but upon Jackson's orders they were summarily hanged. Their execution became an international incident. However, Old Hickory was so busy chasing Spanish leaders from Florida that he did not respond to accusations leveled against him.

Meanwhile, Americans who had poured into the Floridas had prepared claims for damages done to their property by Indians or during time of war. Again the Spanish evacuated Pensacola, this time taking most military forces to Havana.

Sick of the long-drawn Florida contest, Spain entered into a new treaty with the youthful United States. Under its terms, Spain relinquished all claims to Florida. In return, the United States agreed to pay up to five million dollars to U.S. citizens who had claims against Spain.

"It's over!" exclaimed a jubilant James Madison on February 22, 1819, the day Spain formally ceded Florida. He was almost—but not quite—right. The Spanish, French, and British were gone; but the Seminoles remained firmly entrenched in the southeastern tip of the United States of America.

8

Osceola Did Not Touch the Pen

"Charley Emathla and his crowd agreed to go to the West—some time in the next three years. But that means nothing; Osceola did not touch the pen!"

Spreading among Seminole villages by word of mouth, the terse description of action by the man who had emerged as their leader fed the growing fires of hatred between Florida's newly arrived settlers and long-established bands of refugees.

At Payne's Landing on the Ocklawaha River, Col. James Gadsden had pulled off what he considered to be a great coup. After months of negotiation, he persuaded a number of minor chieftains to lead their people out of Florida; they were to go to fertile land in the far West. Since no Seminole could read or write, those who assented to the treaty gave the white man's pen a ceremonial touch of the hand.

Osceola, born about 1800 and never considered by his people to be a chieftain, was the acknowledged leader of those who resisted removal. His tribal name, Asi-yaholo, probably signified "Black Drink Hallooer," or "the warrior who yells loudly after the ceremonial drink of black water."

Legend has it that when commanded to touch the pen with which white men signed the treaty, Osceola obediently moved toward the stump on which the parchment was spread. But when he came within arm's length of the treaty, instead of touching the pen he pulled out his hunting knife and gave a furious stab that cut a great gash in the parchment.

Osceola's anger had been ignited by a band of slave-catchers. While he was away hunting, they reached the village in which he lived and seized Che-cho-ter, one of his wives, as a runaway. They claimed, perhaps correctly, that she was "no real Indian, but mostly black."

Former slaves, largely from Carolina and Georgia, inter-married with warriors who fled from their Creek ancestral hunting grounds. They and their mixed-blood progeny were called by the Creeks "runaways," or Seminoles.

More than two years after East and West Florida came into the possession of the United States by treaty, flags were formally changed at St. Augustine and Pensacola. Gen. Andrew Jackson, who had been named to govern the new American possessions, was present in Pensacola for the July 1821 ceremony. He remained in power for less than a year, until Congress created a new territory from

Osceola in ceremonial dress. [ENGRAVING AFTER PORTRAIT BY GEORGE S. CATLIN]

the two Floridas. Then William P. Duval was sent to govern the still largely unsettled region, which was a mecca for the adventurous and restless of the states to the north. Trouble with the Seminoles was frequent and serious, even during the years in which they had no known leader.

At Payne's Landing in 1833, whites congratulated themselves that they soon would be rid of the Seminoles. Even James Gadsden, who formulated the treaty, seems not to have realized the gravity of Osceola's refusal to touch the pen.

Early in 1835, however, Osceola waylaid Charley Emathla, a petty chieftain who had spoken in favor of removal months earlier and who was now preparing to lead his family out of Florida. Screaming in a fashion that came to be associated with him during battle, Osceola plunged his knife into Emathla's heart.

Gen. Winfield S. Scott, whom subordinates called "Old Fuss and Feathers." [VIRGINIA DEPARTMENT OF ARCHIVES AND HISTORY]

Thirty days later, knowing himself to be a wanted man by white authorities, Osceola waited in ambush for Indian agent Wiley Thompson. Word had reached the Seminoles that white men in Washington had given their approval to plans for immediate removal of all Seminoles from Florida. On December 28, 1835, Thompson and an aide were shot and killed by Osceola. Those who found the bodies did not realize that other events in which Osceola was involved were taking place far away, launching the Second Seminole War.

About the same time Thompson was shot by Osceola, Maj. Francis L. Dade of the U.S. Army noticed what seemed to be suspicious movements in underbrush as he and his 139 men and a six-pound piece of artillery made their march from Tampa to Fort King. Dade's men sang in cadence as they marched over the rough "corduroy" road made of logs, but he signaled for them to halt when two or three palmettos moved almost simultaneously.

Dade had hardly stopped his band, much less managed to arrange them into defensive circles, before a band of about 180 Seminoles struck. Nearly half of his soldiers are believed to have fallen at the first volley from enemy rifles. One man managed successfully to pretend to be dead, and another bribed the Indians to spare his life.

At first these two, the only survivors of Dade's massacre, were not believed when they reached Tampa and told their story. Trying to reconstruct events of the fateful day, authorities concluded that Osceola's murder of Thompson was timed to coincide with the mass killing of Dade's men. Remembered today chiefly by Dade County, named for the man who headed the hapless band, the Dade massacre was one of the bloodiest in U.S. annals.

With full-fledged war now in progress, the Seminoles, who had an estimated two thousand fighting men of Indian, black, and mixed blood, retreated into the swamps. Billy Bowlegs, a seasoned veteran, for a time helped Osceola to plan strategy. In Washington, Gen. Winfield Scott ruefully admitted that after two years of struggle, whites were getting nowhere. So he dispatched to Florida as commander of military troops Virginia-born Gen. Thomas S. Jesup, quartermaster general of the U.S. Army. Jesup had barely reached Florida when Seminoles claimed a new victory in the battle of Wahoo Swamp. They then had the effrontery to make an assault upon strongly fortified Camp Monroe. Defeated there, some of the Seminoles agreed to withdraw south of the Hillsboro River immediately. That region was designated as a staging point from which all Seminoles would be sent to the West. Late in the year, a native warrior friendly to the white man agreed to serve as a runner. He took a message asking Osceola to meet with Gen. Joseph M. Hernandez under a flag of truce.

"I speak as a friend," Hernandez said when Osceola came to him near Fort Peyton late in October 1837. "What induced you to come to me?"

Osceola replied tersely, "We come for good." He then pointed to Coa Hadjo and indicated that this warrior would serve as tribal spokesman.

Hernandez nodded understanding, then became silent. After an interval, he announced, "I wish all of you Seminoles well. But we have been deceived so often that you must come with me. You will get good treatment. You will be glad that you fell into my hands."

As he spoke, the army officer gave a prearranged signal. Before Coa Hadjo, Osceola, and the comrades who accompanied them could seize their loaded guns, nearby forces of Brevet Maj. James A. Ashby appeared from ambush. Concealed in a thicket on Moultrie Creek, they had been within easy gunshot of the Indians who thought they had come to talk peace.

Surgeon Nathan Jarvis, who was present and reported about events of the day, watched Osceola closely. He later said that the great warrior showed no sign of surprise at having been captured under a large white banner that served as an impromptu flag of truce.

Resistance would have meant death. Ashby commanded a force of 250 cavalrymen and dragoons, while

The capture of Osceola, as depicted by a nineteenth-century German artist.

the Seminoles had a total of just fifty-two rifles. They surrendered without firing a shot.

Gen. Thomas Jesup, who had sent a subordinate to carry out the treacherous plan, had in desperation decided to try to trick Osceola by using a flag of truce. Until his death, "the father of the modern quartermaster corps" stoutly defended his actions as "the quickest and easiest way to end a bloody business."

As news of the capture spread over the United States, many of his countrymen denounced Jesup. There was talk in Congress of censure, but nothing came of it. By and large, Americans who knew a little about Florida were happy in their belief that their final and most stubborn foes, the Seminoles, were about to leave at last.

On the day that Osceola was seized, other soldiers also captured about seventy warriors and six women. Cavalrymen forming a hollow phalanx prodded the Seminoles inside and forced them to walk to St. Augustine. There whites turned out en masse to gape and to cheer.

Osceola wore the bright blue calico shirt and red leg-

Billy Bowlegs, one of Osceola's chief aides. [CITY ART MUSEUM, ST. LOUIS]

gings for which he was noted. Having dressed to talk peace, he had a brightly colored shawl over his shoulders and another wrapped around his head. After a period of imprisonment at St. Augustine, he was moved to Fort Moultrie, South Carolina. There the man whom many regard as the greatest of all military strategists among native Americans died at age thirty-four.

Osceola's portrait by George Catlin is in the Smithsonian Institution. A national forest, a state park, three counties, twenty towns, two lakes, and two mountains perpetuate the name of the warrior seized under a flag of truce.

Transplanted New Yorker Isaac H. Bronson led the long fight by which Florida won statehood in 1845, only to secede from the Union sixteen years later.

As for the war launched by Osceola at Christmas 1835, with Seminoles entrenched deep in the Everglades, the final treaty of peace was not signed until 1943. That made the Second Seminole War the longest conflict in the nation's history by far.

PART TWO:
A Nearly Worthless Wilderness

Though part of the United States, Florida still consisted of desolate stretches of swamp and sand dotted with palmettos. Virtually uninhabited except by birds, mosquitoes, alligators, and Seminoles, it was seen as a useful buffer to protect old and established states, as well as a jumping-off place for naval and military action against an old foe.

John James Audubon in the field with gun and dog.

9

John James Audubon Finally Got His Bird

April, 1832

Aboard the cutter Marion
As the "marion" neared the inlet called "Indian Key," my heart swelled with uncontrollable delight. Soon we went off with the deputy collector of the island. Accompanied by him, his pilot, and fisherman, after a short pull we landed on a large key. Few minutes had elapsed when, shot after shot might be heard, and down came whistling through the air the objects of our desire.

Meticulously recording his ornithological adventures, John James Audubon made no secret of the fact that he killed birds in great numbers. Many of them he shot to get their skins that, mounted on wire frames, provided the models for his famous paintings.

By the time the second volume of his now priceless *Birds of America* was published in England, Audubon was a celebrity in his own country. Indeed, his fame helped him gain use of the revenue cutter *Marion* on his Florida visit.

On an 1831 visit to Florida—his first—Audubon did not fare well. Seeking wading birds for inclusion in volume three of his great book, the artist slowly made his way from Charleston to St. Augustine. Sometimes it took six mules to pull his rough wagon. Flies and mosquitoes buzzed about him and continuously nipped at his skin. Birds were plentiful, but extremely wary; he counted it a good day when he bagged one new specimen.

Humans were few and far between. Had the thirty-five thousand or so inhabitants been spread evenly over the peninsula, six people would have occupied each ten square miles. Temperature, insects, and fever plagued the artist and his white spotted dog, Plato, whom Audubon constantly watched, fearful that an alligator might seize the animal.

In St. Augustine, where he considered his room and board payment of $4.50 a week to be exorbitant, he complained that the town was "the poorest hole in Creation." Leaving the Spanish-built town, he headed for Jacksonville (population about six hundred) along the St. Johns River. By the time he reached his destination, both he and Plato were so seasick that they could not stand.

Cutting his visit short, Audubon sailed back to Charleston to recuperate and rest. There he found to his immense delight that the U.S. government was ready to do him a favor. Aboard the smooth sailing revenue cutter that was put at his disposal, he headed for Key West. His prime objective was a bird he earlier had glimpsed only at a great distance: the pink flamingo.

Day after day, he searched without success. Not until

Audubon depicted a Florida heron in the act of eating its catch.

sailing away from Indian Key on May 7, 1832, did he see his first flock of flamingos, causing him to believe that he had "now reached the height of all expectations." His joy was premature; at no time did he find it possible to sail a boat within gunshot of a flock.

Almost, but not quite, as wary as the Flamingo, the sandhill crane, wrote Audubon, would take instant flight "should you accidentally tread on a stick and break it, or suddenly cock your gun." Once he came close enough to a flock to take good aim and fire, "when all the birds instantly flew off greatly alarmed, excepting one which leaped into the air, but immediately came down again, and walked leisurely away with a drooping pinion."

It was this wounded bird that taught him healthy respect for the species. "These birds cannot be approached without caution," he warned, "as their powerful bill is capable of inflicting a severe wound. Knowing this as I do, I would counsel any sportsman not to leave his gun behind, when pursuing a wounded Crane."

Difficult as it was to do so, the artist eventually bagged several cranes, along with half a hundred other kinds of birds he had observed only in Florida. But after a few weeks, during which he discovered the great white heron, he returned to Charleston without the skin of a flamingo.

Capt. Robert Day of the *Marion* promised to try to secure a specimen for him, but that did not satisfy him. Audubon also asked several other new friends to try to kill or purchase a flamingo.

Writing from London in 1837, where he was supervising the printing of his engravings, he made a confession: "I was a great fool not to have gone to Cuba, or sent a person there expressly. It would have cost perhaps one hundred and fifty Dollars, but what is such a sum to the assurance of Truth being had, respecting this remarkable species—unfortunately rare on our Coast?"

Long after having left Florida, the artist finally got his prized bird. Jean Chartrand sent him from Cuba a specimen preserved in rum, along with several dried skins. It was from these that he made for his famous Double Ele-

phant Folio—so named because of its great size—a stu-
pendous painting of a long-legged flamingo with its head
bent close to the water in search of food.

Audubon the outdoorsman and hunter killed in a fashion quite different from Audubon the artist, who bought
specimens he was unable personally to bag. As a hunter,
he shot birds and animals for sport, curiosity, and his next
meal.

When he found a hollow tree that served as a haven for
swallows, Audubon and a companion opened it. He recorded having "caught and killed more than a hundred."
He hunted alligators, rattlesnakes, and cougars. Once he
shot an alligator because he believed a friend would ap-
preciate the hide.

On Coles Island, South Carolina, the artist and his
friends gunned down long-billed curlews for sport. Then
they feasted on oysters, beefsteak, and beverages from
Charleston.

No widely circulated portrait executed during his lifetime depicts Audubon before a canvas with brush in
hand. At least six, including a self-portrait, show him
with a gun, hunting dogs, or both. How did the name of
this mighty hunter become synonymous with "conservation"?

George B. Grinnell, editor of *Forest and Stream* magazine, wanted to stop the wholesale killing of birds for mil-
linery purposes. In 1886 he proposed starting "an
association for the protection of wild birds and their
eggs." In childhood, Grinnell's favorite teacher had been
Mrs. J. J. Audubon, widow of America's greatest wildlife
artist, whose name by then had become universally familiar.

Why not honor his teacher and simultaneously win
members for the "protective association" by dubbing it
the Audubon Society?

Launched as a local movement in New York, it quickly
spread into Massachusetts and Pennsylvania. In 1905,
dozens of local and regional Audubon societies arranged
national merger and incorporation.

Restored, the Audubon House in Key West is open to visitors.

Were he still alive, John James Audubon might be baffled by conservation practices now being advocated in his name. The man who brought the birds and animals of the southeastern United States to life on canvas was a man of his era, a mighty hunter who happened also to be a great artist.

Some of his handiwork, in the form of original engravings from his Birds of America, may be seen at Key West in what was once the home of Capt. John H. Geiger. It was Geiger who served as host to the hunter/artist on his visit to the Florida Keys. Now a public museum, the restored and renamed Audubon House calls for a visit of one to two hours. Among the items offered for sale are posters made from Audubon's prized painting of the pink flamingo. For more information, telephone (305) 294-2116.

10

Stephen Foster Left His Mark

"Danny, you've done it!" exclaimed Bobby Henry of Tampa. "She floats smooth and even!"

Folk arts apprentice Danny Wilcox made no attempt to conceal his delight. "Gotta let Stephen Foster know, right away," he said.

At the Stephen Foster State Folk Culture Center in White Springs, news that Danny had successfully completed a Seminole dugout canoe meant another big victory. As recently as the 1960s a few Seminoles still used the canoes during alligator hunting trips into the Everglades. By 1980 the centuries-old art of laboriously digging out a canoe from a cypress log was almost extinct. Funded partly by a grant from the National Endowment for the Humanities, persons working under Florida's secretary of state, Jim Smith, set out to save the ancient skill, almost in the fashion that environmentalists seek to save a fast-vanishing bird or animal species.

Bobby Henry learned to make canoes from his father. When he was very young, he remembers, he and his father would scan many big trees in search of just the right one. For a canoe, the standing cypress had to be six or seven feet in diameter at the base and at least four feet wide— but not much more—at the top.

"Soon as we'd found the right tree, my father would take out his axe," Henry recalls. "Maybe five feet up the trunk, he'd ring that tree with the axe. But even with a big strip of bark gone, it would take that old cypress nearly a year to die."

Once dead, it took two or three days to fell the tree so that it landed on logs that kept it from going into swamp water. Cut to proper length, no more than twenty feet and no less than fifteen feet, the log was stripped of all bark. "That's when the real job of making a dugout begins," according to Henry. "You have to burn out the inside; no one could ever chop it out properly with an axe. And it won't burn like you want it to, unless you control the fire with mud packs."

With the main body of wood slowly removed by burning, the craftsman resorts to a big axe. Then he turns to an adz for final smoothing and shaping.

"Got to float her every few days while she's being finished," explains Tampa's Bobby Henry. "You want a canoe that sits level in the water. And it has to be as light as possible—with a good sturdy hull maybe three inches thick, while the sides ought not to be more than one inch thick."

In the lifetime of Henry, who is one of the few living persons who can remember daily, almost casual, use of the dugout canoe, the vessel has become a symbol of the Seminole past. Almost as soon as he agreed to teach Danny Wilcox the craft of making a dugout, he made plans to float the new canoe in a small swamp at Tampa's Seminole Village.

Miles to the north, near the Georgia/Florida state line, workers at the center Henry tersely calls "Stephen Foster" placed detailed records in the Florida Folklife archive. Photographs and verbal descriptions are sufficiently exact, they are sure, to make it possible for a skilled workman to create a dugout years or decades in the future.

Stephen Foster, perhaps the best known of America's ballad composers, never set foot in Florida. It is unlikely that the Pennsylvania native was ever within a three days' journey of the peninsula. Yet no other spot in the nation commemorates him in a fashion quite like that of the folk culture center that bears his name.

Foster's name appears on the map of Florida parks and

museums because of an almost accidental decision on his part. In 1851 the Pittsburgh native wrote "Swanee River" deliberately modifying the spelling and pronunciation of *Suwannee* for better euphony of the lyrics.

At about the age of fifteen, Foster briefly attended a "college" where he was fascinated with music. He had already taught himself to play the guitar and banjo and had done some composing. Since his relatives did not think a musical career would be suitable for him, they sent him to Cincinnati to be a bookkeeper.

Dialect songs were then all the rage, so Stephen soon began to compose for black-face performers. He sold some of his better works to New York publisher Edwin P. Christy, who paid him ten dollars per composition for all performing rights. In at least two cases he allowed an extra five dollars for permission to attach his own name to Foster's work.

Stephen's brother Morrison, who later became his business manager, gave a detailed account of how Foster's most popular song took shape. "One day in 1851, Stephen came into my office and said to me: 'What's a good name of two syllables for a Southern river?'" He needed that name for use in a new version of a song earlier made public under the title of "Old Folks at Home."

Foster was deliberately trying to get away from "Ethiopian" dialect and style. Yet in order to be useful on the music hall stage, a song should focus upon a southern— not a northern—river. He didn't even consider the Monongahela, in spite of the fact that he had been familiar with it since childhood.

When Morrison Foster suggested that Mississippi's Yazoo River "has a good musical sound," Stephen shook his head. "It has already been used, and everybody knows the song," he said. Morrison then mentioned the Pee Dee, which flows through North and South Carolina.

Stephen Foster actually wrote and briefly used lines that invite listeners to "visit" a spot "'Way down upon the Pedee River." But it did not produce the reaction he wanted.

The Suwanee River, as depicted by a nineteenth-century artist.

Morrison dutifully opened an atlas and began searching for a suitable river. When he came to Suwannee, his brother delightedly cried, "That's it!" On the spot, according to Morrison, "He wrote the name down and the song was finished—commencing with " 'Way down upon the Swanee River.' "

The title page of sheet music published by Christy described Foster's song as "An Ethiopian Melody, Written and Composed by E. P. Christy." In 1852 it was called "one of the most successful songs that has ever appeared in any country. Publishers keep two presses running on it, and sometimes three, yet they cannot supply the demand."

At a time when the sale of five thousand copies was considered great, "Old Folks" sold 150,000 copies in two years. Englishmen as well as Americans sang about the river with the melodic name. Letters written by soldiers in the Crimean War said that the sentimental song by an American was one of two favorites among fighting men.

Stephen Collins Foster died on January 13, 1864, in New York City. A penniless wanderer whose wife had left him, he had no idea that a region he'd never visited would help to keep his memory fresh or that "Swanee River" would become the Florida state song.

Rising in Ware County, Georgia, the Suwannee River flows about 240 miles to the Gulf of Mexico. Floridians who conceived the idea of seeking state support for a folk culture center insisted from the first that it should be built at a spot on the river not far south of the Georgia state line.

Thelma A. Boltin helped to launch at the Stephen Foster Center one of the nation's largest annual folk festivals. Since its inception in 1952, it has become a model for numerous other states.

> Cheese and cornbread on the shelf
> If you want any more come see for yourself!

That invitation conjures up images of corn shuck chair bottoms, pine needle baskets of Creek Indians, and dugout canoes such as those made by Danny Wilcox under the supervision of Bobby Henry. But native American artifacts, music, dance, drama, customs, and food make up only a part of the Stephen Foster Center's offering. Florida is one of the nation's most diverse regions, in terms of the cultural heritage of those who live there. Were he alive to visit and to listen, Stephen Foster surely would rejoice that the center bearing his name brings together and preserves folk culture from a dozen nations.

Memorial Day weekend, the time of the annual statewide festival, is the best time to visit Stephen Foster State Folk Culture Center. A stay of two or three days is indicated at this season. But at any season, the center is good for several hours of browsing among dioramas and other exhibits that depict scenes described in some of Foster's most famous songs. For additional information, address inquiries to P. O. Drawer G, White Springs, FL 32906; telephone (904) 397-3733.

11

No One Knew What to Expect of Edmund K. Smith, or His State

To all citizens of the Trans-Mississippi:
YOUR HOMES ARE IN PERIL
VIGOROUS ACTION ON YOUR PART CAN ALONE
SAVE PORTIONS OF YOUR STATE FROM INVASION
You must contest the advance of the enemy,
thicket, gulley, and stream,
HARASS HIS REAR, AND CUT OFF HIS SUPPLIES
—*Edmund Kirby-Smith, Major General, C.S.A.*

In late September 1863, hastily printed posters appeared in most major Texas cities and in Confederate-held centers in both Arkansas and Louisiana. Although the Indian Territory was not a state, a few of Smith's fervent notices were posted even there, in present-day Oklahoma.

Loss of Little Rock, Arkansas, to Federal troops prompted the last-ditch plea by the native of St. Augustine. Virtually cut off from Richmond and too far west to be a target of major action by Union armies, the Trans-Mississippi Department of the C.S.A. had only one real authority: Smith. He was in civil as well as military command, which he executed with such fervor that great numbers of people cursed the region as "Kirby-Smithdom."

Smith's immediate subordinates, accustomed to his mercurial ways, were not surprised to be called to his tent a few weeks after it was apparent that his plea for a civilian uprising had fallen upon deaf ears.

"Thank you for coming at this hour of the night," their commander began after having told aides to be at ease.

61

"You no doubt surmise that we are about to launch a major movement against the enemy.

"I deeply regret that no such plans are on foot. Instead, I must tell you that I have been wrestling with personal issues. I have reached a decision, and you must be the first to know.

"When you leave this tent tonight, I shall take off my uniform—forever."

According to orally transmitted accounts of the strangest staff meeting of the Civil War, Smith's subordinates were too taken aback to protest. Finally one of them ventured to ask, "Sir, what has prompted this extraordinary decision?"

"Providence," Smith replied firmly. "My eyes have been opened. The fight is nearly over. God is the intervening power. It is His hand that has strengthened the enemy."

He paused, eyed his subordinates uncertainly, then continued, "In exchange for my uniform, I shall put on a round collar—after having entered holy orders."

The stunned Confederate officers had little to say to one another as they left the staff meeting. Their commander was known to be devout and subject to swift changes of mind. Some subordinates compared him with his native state and said, "Sometimes it's hard to know whether Florida—or Kirby-Smith—is in this war for real, or is just playing a game."

Clearly no game, his decision to give up the gray-clad army he commanded to enter the army of the Lord did not stick. He seems to have worn civilian clothing for only a few days as he went through the motions of turning over his command. Then the news that his ships had successfully run the Union blockade at Galveston and had arrived with much-needed machinery was taken as another message from heaven.

"Providence has spoken again," he said. "My announcement was premature. I shall fight until the glorious Second American Revolution has been won. Then, and only then, I will take off my uniform forever and enter the ministry."

With machinery brought from England in exchange for cotton he had sent in packet ships, Smith hastily built factories that soon began turning out substantial quantities of ammunition and a few light weapons. He established vitally needed salt works and began systematic shipments to salt-starved Confederate states east of the Mississippi River.

About six months after his brief interval out of uniform, Smith was promoted to the rank of general. Hastily mobilized troops under his command were victorious in the Red River campaign. In its aftermath, soldiers in gray, along with a few units of American Indian allies, pursued Union Gen. Nathaniel P. Banks all the way to the Mississippi River.

Paradoxically, the Florida man who briefly believed that Providence wanted him to quit the fight was the last Confederate commander to lay down arms. Through a

Soldiers of Smith's Trans-Mississippi Army.
[PICTORIAL HISTORY OF THE CONFEDERACY]

subordinate, he surrendered on May 26, 1865, signaling that the Civil War was finally completely ended.

In Florida, where few persons got fresh or accurate accounts of Smith's activities, public sentiment was chaotic and mixed. After all, the state itself was—like Smith—of two contradictory minds.

Admitted to statehood on March 3, 1845, Florida remained in the Union just under sixteen years, then seceded in January 1861. The only change in the constitution was the substitution of "Confederate States" for "United States."

During the frenzied week before the secession convention met at Tallahassee, Rebels had seized Fort Marion, Fort Clinch, and the arsenal at Apalachicola.

Then on active duty in Texas, Major Edmund Kirby Smith—he later adopted a hyphenated surname in honor of his mother—did not get the news from home until March 1861, when he angrily refused to turn Camp Colorado over to units of the Texas militia. Almost simultaneously with that decision, he resigned his commission to return to Florida to become a colonel of cavalry. Rapidly advancing in rank, he became chief of staff to

C.S.A. Gen. Edmund Kirby Smith [KEENE ARCHIVES]

Gen. Joseph E. Johnston and helped to organize the Confederate Army of the Shenandoah.

Meanwhile, in Florida one Federal installation after another surrendered or was seized. Yet the immense region was never fully under Confederate control. At the time the opening guns of the Civil War were fired, Union forces held only three installations in the entire southeast, outside of Charleston harbor. All three were in Florida: Fort Pickens, off Pensacola Bay; Fort Taylor, at Key West; and Fort Jefferson, in the Dry Tortugas Islands. With a population of 140,000—less than one-tenth that of Virginia—the sparsely settled peninsula became a haven for both Union and Confederate deserters.

An active pro-Union underground flourished in Florida throughout the war, yet Tallahassee was the only Confederate capital that did not fall to Federal forces. An underground group in the capital never did concede that secession of the state was legal. May 1864 saw a convention of Unionists meet at Jacksonville and name delegates to attend the upcoming Republican national convention. One of their formal resolutions declared, in part, "Here, we feel like horse-traders struggling in the waters of the Mississippi—that it is a mighty poor time to swap horses; therefore, Abraham Lincoln is the choice of this convention for the next President of the United States."

Five months after Florida's most colorful Confederate general surrendered, another state convention assembled at Tallahassee. Delegates repealed the ordinance of secession and—without submitting the document to popular vote, adopted a new constitution. Shortly afterward, President Andrew Johnson formally proclaimed that "the insurrection which heretofore existed in the State of Florida is at an end, and is henceforth to be so regarded."

Neither General Smith nor anyone else anticipated that Florida soon again would be known as "the ideal place for important prisoners" and would be pivotal in the high-stakes political game that ended Reconstruction of the war-torn South.

12

Slaves of Key West Were First to Be Freed by Edict

Key West   August, 1862
  *Slavery cannot exist here and does not at this moment.
There is not a negro lawfully held to service in Key West.*

  *An uprising of slaves would not be permitted, but a
slave can declare himself free, refuse to work, and still be
protected by martial law; for it does not recognize slavery
any more than it does secession. The master cannot
punish a slave without committing an offense against
martial law.*

—The New Era

It was not strange that editorial comments in the
abolition newspaper of Key West should use language that
sometimes seemed contradictory, stressing freedom, yet
frequently referring to slavery. Freedom by military edict
was a new idea whose time—insisted Abraham Lincoln,
among many others—had not yet come.

Tempestuous Gen. David Hunter, U.S.A., had other
ideas. For twenty years prior to the outbreak of war, the
West Point graduate served in minor positions on the
western frontier. He became a colonel of cavalry on May
14, 1861; three days later he was made a brigadier general.

Sent south after promotion to the rank of major general,
Hunter was given command of the entire Department of
the South. On May 9, 1862, he published a formal edict.
Having surveyed the vast region in which Federal martial
law was supposed to be effective, Hunter declared that
"slavery and martial law are incompatible." He then proceeded to declare that all persons in his department—

David Hunter, major general of volunteers, U.S.A. [PHOTOGRAPHIC HISTORY OF THE CIVIL WAR]

Georgia, South Carolina, and Florida—who were then held as slaves were, by his order, made free persons.

It took ten days for news of his action to reach Washington. Once he heard of Hunter's proclamation and digested its import, President Abraham Lincoln revoked his general's order. Himself working on a preliminary draft of a proclamation designed to free slaves in rebellious territory, the president had no intention of being upstaged by one of his own generals.

Since much of the region over which Hunter exercised nominal authority was firmly Confederate, even before Lincoln countermanded the emancipation edict, local authorities in Georgia and South Carolina simply ignored it.

In badly divided Florida, there was one spot where Confederates never managed to gain control: Key West. Several hundred slaves lived in and about the town, and Federal authorities governed it while Florida seceded from the Union and began sending troops to fight for the South.

Ignoring instructions from Washington, Gen. Alfred H. Terry relayed General Hunter's edict to the southernmost tip of the Florida peninsula. There the commandant, Colonel Morgan of the Forty-eighth New York Infantry, proceeded to make emancipation effective immediately.

Joshua, a slave of about age forty, was spokesman for one group of blacks who said they did not want their freedom. Their masters took good care of them, said Joshua, and they preferred to make no change in their situation. "No matter," ruled Morgan. "You must leave the plantations at once. That is a military order which will be enforced at gunpoint, if necessary. Whether you like it or not, you men are free!"

Furious at Abraham Lincoln's actions in countermanding his edict, David Hunter, a native of the District of Columbia who knew his way around there, pulled strings in Congress. By congressional action he was given authority to raise black troops and to use them in combat. So it was the man whose proclamation proved effective only in remote Key West recruited and drilled men to make up the First and Second South Carolina Volunteers.

The nation's first black military companies made up of former slaves were headed by white officers: Col. Thomas W. Higginson and Col. James Montgomery. As soon as their men were in shape to fight, they led them into Florida. With them, they took an amended order from Hunter. Under its terms, they were instructed:

> [to] occupy Jacksonville and to carry the Proclamation of Freedom to the enslaved; to call all loyal men into the service of the United States; to occupy as much of the State of Florida as possible; and to neglect no means consistent with the usages of civilized warfare to weaken, harass, and annoy those who are in rebellion against the United States.

When Abraham Lincoln's Emancipation Proclamation was issued on January 1, 1863, it created fresh problems in Key West. An earlier act had ordered the confiscation of property (which included slaves) used in "aiding, abetting, or promoting" war against the Union. That clearly exempted slaves belonging to loyal, or unionist, owners. In Key West the property rights of such owners were respected. Lincoln's proclamation applied only to regions in a state of rebellion, and Key West was, and always had been, firmly in Federal control.

The first real battle in which black soldiers took part was at Port Hudson, Louisiana. [NINETEENTH-CENTURY LITHOGRAPH]

A number of Key West slaves belonging to men loyal to the Union appear to have remained in slavery, while comrades who had been the property of Rebels were freed under the terms of David Hunter's edict. The latter, first in the nation to be freed by edict, left their former masters nearly six months before Lincoln's proclamation was issued.

Numerous black military units, perhaps as many as a dozen, poured into Florida when Federal recruitment of former slaves became official and active. Governor John Milton mourned that Federal officials intended to reduce the state to "a waste, a howling wilderness, colonized with negroes."

Black troops did sometimes go on raiding expeditions in East Florida, where they allegedly obeyed the orders of white leaders and shot down defenseless civilians in the streets. In West Florida they captured and sacked the villages of Marianna and Eucheanna.

Union Gen. Rufus Saxton strongly defended Florida blacks who became members of his army. "They will fight with as much desperation as any people in the World," said an official summary of March 6, 1863. "There is pres-

Done at the city of Washington, this first day of
January, in the year of our Lord one thousand
eight hundred and sixty three, and of the

Independence of the United States
of America the eighty-seventh.

Abraham Lincoln

By the President;
  William H Seward,
    Secretary of State

ently a great scarcity of muskets. If this want is supplied, it is my opinion that the entire State of Florida can be rescued from the enemy and made into an asylum for persons from other States who are freed from bondage by the Proclamation."

Saxton's hopes were premature. Although Jacksonville, St. Augustine, and other centers fell to Federal troops, Confederates often recaptured towns and forts held for a few months by men in blue, and they maintained a strong hold upon the Gulf coast throughout the conflict. Only Key West was unequivocally under Federal control from start to finish. Hence it was only there that Gen. David Hunter's emancipation edict was fully implemented and never revoked, even when Abraham Lincoln countermanded it.

An obscure figure overshadowed by commanders who fought major battles and led well-known campaigns, David Hunter is seldom mentioned in accounts of the conflict that split Florida and the nation asunder. But Rufus and his comrades who were forced to accept freedom whether they were ready for it or not, along with hosts of other blacks clamoring for escape from their masters, never forgot the sixty-one-year-old general who was first to emancipate slaves.

13

Judah P. Benjamin Weighed All Options, Then Fled to Florida

"Mr. President, is your decision firm?"

"It is," replied Jefferson Davis, head of the crumbling Confederate States of America. "There is still a chance that I can rally enough troops in the West to mount another campaign."

"Then, sir, I must bid you adieu," said Judah P. Benjamin. Until thirty days earlier he had functioned as secretary of state of the C.S.A. That made him almost as much a wanted man as Davis. Both men knew that he had carefully considered the options and had concluded that the only reasonable chance of escape was in fleeing to Florida.

Both leaders knew that every major port would be carefully watched. So long as prominent members of the Confederate government remained at large, the Federal blockade of southern ports would mean the likely stopping of European-bound vessels to search them for fugitives.

Partly to avoid the risk of taking to sea, but primarily because he still hoped to transform the fight in the west, Jefferson Davis had plotted a circuitous overland route. He planned to move from North Carolina, through South Carolina, and into Georgia.

Once in that state, he hoped to travel swiftly to the southern edge. He would then proceed across Alabama and Mississippi, always avoiding cities and major towns, to the Mississippi River.

Benjamin, a long-time favorite of Davis and the only

Judah P. Benjamin
[LESLIE'S ILLUSTRATED
WEEKLY]

Jew to hold cabinet rank in either of the warring American governments, spent more than a week arguing against Davis's proposed course of action. On the flight from Richmond, which began on April 1, 1865, he had spent many hours poring over maps.

"Florida is the logical place to go," he began insisting as the presidential party moved from Greensboro, North Carolina, toward Abbeville, South Carolina. "It is sparsely populated, and the bulk of the people there are our solid supporters. In the back country, we can hide out for weeks, then take a small ship to Cuba or one of the Caribbean Islands, there to wait for transportation on a British vessel not subject to search."

His argument made so much sense that Jefferson Davis wavered for a day or two. In the end he rejected Benjamin's plan because it had no provision for attempting to raise new troops, a prospect that his secretary of state considered impracticable.

Other members of Davis's party were satisfied to be guided by the judgment of their ex-president. So emotions ran high on the afternoon of May 3 when, on the west bank of the Savannah River, Judah P. Benjamin told his leader and comrades goodbye.

Accompanied only by Capt. H. J. Leovy, who had already practiced addressing his companion as Monsieur Bonfals, Benjamin headed due south. "We must move rapidly, but not too rapidly," the man now calling himself a Frenchman told his companion.

Just two days out of Richmond, he had started to grow a beard. Now full, it concealed the features that were described on "wanted" posters distributed by Federal troops. Goggles, a cloak made in European style, and a heavy black hat completed the disguise.

C.S.A. President Jefferson Davis

Benjamin's appearance and route enabled him to ride the entire length of Georgia without once being stopped for interrogation. By the time he reached the Georgia/Florida line, he heard rumors that Jefferson Davis and his entire party had been captured near Irwinville, Georgia.

Once on Florida soil, Monsieur Bonfals became Joseph Pinckney, a decayed aristocrat from South Carolina who was seeking land upon which to relocate. His beard was trimmed, his hat and goggles were discarded, and homespun clothing purchased from a farmer was donned.

May 15 brought a special sense of elation. Having crossed the Suwannee River that day, he regarded himself as in a safe haven. However, he knew it would take several more days of hard riding to reach a spot where he could hide until the furor about his escape subsided.

Confederates had never lost control of the Gulf coast; so the astute fugitive turned toward Tampa. There he found a friend in Maj. John Lesley, who triumphantly led him to a splendid mansion on the Manatee River.

"It was built by members of the Gamble family," explained Lesley. "They used tabby, and used it well."

Judah's puzzled expression caused his friend to offer an explanation. "Tabby is a special Florida version of concrete," he explained. "Oyster shells are burned to produce lime. Then the lime and sand, plus more oyster shells, are mixed to make a splendid mortar that sets as hard as the finest concrete."

Even though he now had a rough idea of how the exterior of his hiding place might look, the former cabinet member was not prepared for what he found. To his astonishment the Gamble mansion was two stories tall and had eighteen splendid pillars around three sides. When he first glimpsed it in the distance, he learned from Lesley that it had been the center for a 3,500-acre sugar plantation.

"Excellent!" exclaimed the fugitive. "I shall be very much at home here; in Louisiana, I own a sugar plantation—unless it has been seized by the Federals."

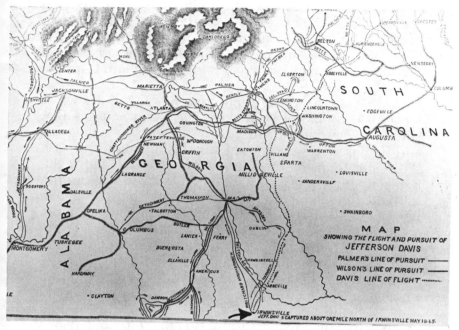

MAP
SHOWING THE FLIGHT AND PURSUIT OF
JEFFERSON DAVIS
PALMER'S LINE OF PURSUIT ———
WILSON'S LINE OF PURSUIT ———
DAVIS' LINE OF FLIGHT ·············

JEFF. DAVIS CAPTURED ABOUT ONE MILE NORTH OF IRWINSVILLE MAY 10-65.

Jefferson Davis and his party were captured in Georgia a day or two before Judah P. Benjamin reached Florida in safety.

Now calling himself Mr. Howard, Benjamin found life in the mansion built by Robert Gamble so comfortable that he considered giving up his plan to seek refuge in England.

Still, his host—the new owner of the mansion— noticed that Mr. Howard spent a great deal of time on the upstairs veranda. With a splendid brass spyglass in hand, he kept continual watch upon the river.

In spite of his vigilance, he failed to spot members of a surprise Federal raiding party until they were almost upon him. Barely ahead of soldiers who had no idea that a member of the Confederate cabinet was in central Florida, Benjamin managed to get across the Manatee River without being seen and followed.

He then found refuge in the home of Capt. Frederick

Tresca, who had become intimately familiar with coastal waters during years as a blockade runner. Tresca had heard that a yawl had been sunk in a creek to conceal it from Federal marauders. He made inquiries, discovered the rumor to be correct, and persuaded Captain Currie to raise the vessel.

On May 23 the yawl, dingy from months under water, moved slowly out of Whittaker's Bayou on Sarasota Bay. Hiding by day and moving slowly at night, the tiny vessel and its passengers reached Knight's Key about July 10. With gold from the money belt he wore day and night, Benjamin hired a seagoing vessel that took him to Bimini.

Tradition asserts that once he reached Bimini, the man who was en route to England to practice law solemnly consulted a compass to find the direction toward Washington, D.C. Then he vigorously thumbed his nose and climbed aboard a ship bound for Liverpool.

The subject of a frenzied manhunt that extended throughout the nation and into Canada, Benjamin managed to spend nearly sixty days in comfort in Florida, much of that time in a mansion. No other top Confederate leader had a comparable experience in attempting to escape from Federal troops.

"Benjamin's hiding place" is the only remaining ante-bellum plantation house in south Florida. Situated at Ellenton—three miles from Palmetto and five miles from Bradenton—it has been completely restored and is now owned by the state and used as the centerpiece of the Gamble Plantation State Historic Site. Plan to devote about one and one-half hours for a tour of the mansion and grounds. Address inquiries to the Judah P. Benjamin Confederate Memorial, 3708 Patten Avenue, Ellenton, FL 33532; telephone (813) 722-1017.

14

"Devil's Island of the West" Held Dr. Samuel Mudd and Companions

Courtroom, Washington, D.C.
June 30, 1865, 10 o'clock A.M.
The Commission met, with closed doors, pursuant to adjournment.
All the members present; also the Judge Advocate and the Assistant Judge Advocates.
The Commission do hereby sentence the said Samuel A. Mudd to be imprisoned at hard labor for life, at such place as the President shall direct.
The Commission thereupon adjourned sine die.

David Hunter,
Major General of Volunteers

Hunter, a Washington celebrity since having abolished slavery in Key West months before the Emancipation Proclamation was issued, had been the talk of the capital for days. Everyone knew that as head of a special nine-man commission named to try captured conspirators charged with Lincoln's murder, Hunter would have great impact upon the decisions.

Most people in the capital applauded early news that four conspirators had been sentenced to die. David E. Herold, George A. Atzerodt, and Lewis Payne were considered to be "guilty beyond a shadow of a doubt" of having aided and abetted John Wilkes Booth. A minority of civilians questioned the scheduled execution of Mrs. Mary E. Surratt.

It was the leniency of the court—not its harshness—that angered many ordinary folk. Was it not beyond dis-

"Lincoln conspirators" who were secretly shipped to Florida for imprisonment escaped the fate of the four who were hanged.

pute that Dr. Samuel Mudd had set the broken leg of the man who shot the president? Yet he, along with co-conspirators sentenced earlier, would get off lightly. Instead of hanging with the rest, they would spend their lives at hard labor.

The constitutionality of the trial of civilians by a panel of six generals and three judges is widely questioned today. In 1865 only the attorneys who represented the defendants dared to raise any questions.

Feelings against Dr. Samuel A. Mudd ran especially high. The son of a wealthy slave-holding family and a known critic of Abraham Lincoln, the physician from Charles City, Maryland, was believed to have been part of the assassination conspiracy from the beginning. Generations later, Mudd's name would be cleared, largely through the influence of a descendant, television newsman Roger Mudd.

In 1865 high-placed national leaders were furious that Mudd did not hang—along with four others—at the Old Penitentiary in Washington. To make matters worse, in the considered view of Secretary of War Edwin M. Stanton, Mudd and others who escaped the rope were to be confined in the prison at Albany, New York. Selection of that site was made by President Andrew Johnson.

Tradition insists that Stanton sent for General Hunter a few days before the shackled and hooded prisoners were to be transferred to New York.

"You know Florida well," Stanton is believed to have said. "New York is far too settled, too heavily populated. To make sure that the prisoners will not get help, they must go to Florida—but where?"

Hunter did not hesitate.

"Send them to the Devil's Island of the west," he suggested. "There is no hope of escape from the place—and very little hope for the living who find themselves there.

"Perhaps you know the place I mean," Hunter continued. "If you do not, I should tell you that Fort Jefferson is totally inaccessible except by heavy gunboats.

"During the late unpleasantness, we used the fort as a prison for captured deserters. Not a man left the place alive, except for those whose sentences were commuted."

Secretary Stanton made secret arrangements with the captain of the gunboat U.S.S. *Florida*. Sailing under sealed orders, the ship that carried the convicted men moved south, not toward New York.

Not until after he passed Hilton Head, South Carolina, did Captain Budd reveal to crew members that their destination was a group of seven tiny islands sixty miles west of Florida's southern tip, discovered long ago by Ponce de León. Because they lacked fresh water but abounded in turtles, Americans called them the Dry Tortugas.

Very early, a few visionary strategists had insisted that the islands were of tremendous importance. A stout fort erected there would virtually control shipping in that part of the Gulf of Mexico, they said.

So engineers started work on Fort Jefferson soon after Florida became a U.S. territory. With walls eight feet thick and fifty feet high, it had three gun tiers designed to hold 450 heavy guns.

Even during the years in which most of Florida was in Confederate hands, Fort Jefferson remained a federal garrison. When the first captured deserters were sent there to serve prison sentences, someone erected a crudely scrawled greeting borrowed from Dante's *Inferno*, ALL HOPE ABANDON, YE WHO ENTER HERE. Initially, many who were sent there were glad to go because their death sentences had been commuted by Abraham Lincoln.

Soon, though, the seventy-foot moat was seen to be infested with man-eating sharks, which were fearful enough, but yellow fever was worse. With a normal prison population of about six hundred men, Fort Jefferson saw burial details at work almost every day of every week.

Dr. Samuel Mudd, Edward Spangler, Samuel Arnold, and Michael O'Laughlin were greeted with catcalls by prisoners when they shuffled into Fort Jefferson. For the most part, even military deserters hated men convicted of participating in the assassination of Lincoln. So the newly arrived civilian prisoners were put into sequestered cells to prevent other inmates from harming them.

Wearing gray flannel overalls and moving awkwardly because of the chains about their legs, Mudd and his companions were initially permitted only one or two hours a day of exercise in a yard. At night they slept on the bare wooden floor.

The hard labor to which they had been sentenced for life proved to be less dreadful than they had feared. Because of his medical skill, Mudd was assigned to the prison hospital, where many had died.

Another of the Lincoln conspirators drew an assignment to the carpentry shop. O'Laughlin was set to work cleaning bricks, and Arnold landed an easy job in the office of the provost marshal. Mudd and Arnold were permitted to work without wearing ball and chain, and their comrades were soon told that they would have them taken off at night.

Food at the most formidable prison on U.S. soil was worse than that aboard globe-encircling sailing vessels.

U.S. Secretary of War
Edwin M. Stanton [U.S.
SIGNAL CORPS]

Many men who escaped malaria and yellow fever came down with scurvy and were sent to the hospital to be tended by Dr. Mudd.

Mudd's companion, Arnold, described Fort Jefferson years after his sentence was commuted. He remembered it as a place of flies, mosquitoes, rotten meat, unbearable heat and humidity, the constant smell of dysentery, and total hopelessness. Death was soon as the only way out, and many inmates found diversion in tossing bits of tainted meat to sharks in the moat.

In Washington there was a flurry of excitement when word came—erroneous, as it proved—that ex-Confederates planned to liberate the prisoners held in Florida. At Fort Jefferson, Mudd and his companions never even heard such rumors. They correctly assumed that nothing short of a major naval assault would pose a challenge to their captors.

In 1868 yellow fever threatened to overcome the garrison. In this crisis the death of the last U.S. Army surgeon stationed there placed Samuel Mudd in a critical position. He hesitated only briefly, then offered his services to try to save his captors as well as their captives.

When the fever was finally contained, grateful officers drafted a petition. Addressed to the president of the United States and requesting that Mudd be pardoned, it reached Washington a few weeks before Ulysses S. Grant was to be inaugurated.

Andrew Johnson, who may never have given his approval to the transfer of the Lincoln conspirators to Florida, signed papers that ordered the release of heroic Dr. Samuel Mudd. Shortly afterward, just before he relinquished the White House to his successor, he ordered the release of Mudd's three companions.

Johnson's pardon promised freedom for men whose guilt was debatable even by the standards of a hastily convened military tribunal. The presidential action came too late to help Michael O'Laughlin, who was among the scores of victims of yellow fever whom Mudd was unable to save.

Now the centerpiece of Fort Jefferson National Monument, the prison in which the Lincoln conspirators were confined is accessible by seaplane from Key West. Most people who visit it leave with fresh understanding of why it was the only major Federal military installation in the entire South that never fell into Confederate hands.

For seaplane reservations, contact Key West Seaplane Service, 5603 West Junior College Road, telephone (305) 294-6978. General information about the infamous place of detention is available from the Superintendent, Everglades National Park, Box 279, Homestead, FL 33030.

PART THREE:
No More Fear of Spain

Spanish influence remained prominently visible, notably in St. Augustine. Many Americans feared that the chaos created by civil war would lead Spain to reclaim the region. Instead, settlers flocked to Florida in increasing numbers and made it permanently American. The peninsula served as the outpost from which Americans went to the Spanish-American War, which established the United States as a world power.

John Wallace, for twelve years a member of the Florida legislature. [CARPETBAGGERS IN FLORIDA]

15

John Wallace Declared That Struggle Made Florida Stronger

Tallahassee, 1876
My design is to correct the impression that former slaves, when enfranchised, had no conception of good government, and, therefore their chief ambition was corruption and plunder.

Enslaved for more than 200 years, their constant contact with a more enlightened race would have made them better citizens and more honest legislators if they had not been contaminated by strange white men who represented themselves as their saviors.

—John Wallace

A self-taught ex-slave from North Carolina, Wallace published a vivid account of carpetbaggers in Florida as an indictment of whites who flocked there to profit from postwar chaos.

"My escape from slavery came during the period when Gen. Ambrose Burnside's campaigns had much of North Carolina in turmoil," he explained. "Washington, D.C. seemed the right place to go. I did not then know that slavery was still legal there.

"When I heard that the Second U.S. Colored Troops was being raised, I immediately volunteered. Most of my two and one-half years in uniform were spent in Florida. That persuaded me to take up residence in Tallahassee upon my discharge from the military upon Jan. 1, 1866."

Like Wallace, many of the nearly fifty thousand persons who had poured into Florida during the war chose to remain. Land was plentiful and cheap; the climate was unequaled. Its climate persuaded Harriet Beecher Stowe and a few other New Englanders to build winter homes along the St. Johns River and to begin spending months there each year.

Some of the newcomers were graduates of Ivy League colleges. Many had received good educations, but only the self-taught ex-slave put together a detailed, though sometimes tedious, account of events during the turbulent decades of Reconstruction.

"Black troops found fine opportunities for military service in Florida," Wallace often said in his public speeches, "but the state never saw any really hard fighting. Our ports were damaged or destroyed, and the railroads we were starting to build were torn up. Some of the white officers and men who were stationed at Federal posts were surprised to find Florida such a pleasant place to live; they began encouraging friends to visit, and the tourist industry got started."

March 1867 saw all Florida restored to military rule. Republicans seized control of most civilian posts and, with the help of the Freedmen's Bureau, largely operated the state for years.

Slaves acted prematurely by organizing in Tallahassee late in 1866. Joseph Oats, formerly a slave of Governor Walker, was elected to Congress by blacks—2,000 or more in number—who held a rally under the protection of Federal troops.

In a lengthy speech delivered at Houstoun's Spring, Oats said he had been to Washington and had conferred with the president. "You have true friends in Washington," he told his enthralled listeners.

They contributed several hundred dollars to help him defray expenses of another trip to the nation's capital. "It was believed, however, that Oats did not go further than Savannah, where he had a good time, spent the freedmen's money, and returned home," according to a contemporary report.

Wallace considered the Oats incident to be in a class by itself. "Ex-slaves showed that they could govern as well as be governed," he said many times.

Named to serve as a messenger at the constitutional convention of 1868, Wallace was elected constable of Leon County upon adoption of the new state constitution. After two years as constable, he waged a successful campaign for a seat in the legislature, where he spent twelve years.

It was as a member of the legislature that Wallace was a close observer of the course of Reconstruction.

Because of the Federal military presence, Republicans were able to maintain nominal control. But the heavily Democratic legislature managed to enact statute after statute intended to put free and enfranchised blacks into economic and political slavery.

Voter interest was at times lower than in any other former Confederate region. In an important statewide election only eleven thousand whites and fifteen thousand blacks bothered to go to the polls, in spite of the permanent population's having jumped past two hundred thousand.

State land held in trust to guarantee the interest and principal on railway bonds issued by Florida became the target of the greedy. Timber, rather than the land itself, was the prize. White Republicans arranged to sell 1.1 million acres to the New York and Florida Lumber Company at ten cents an acre. To compound the enormity of the land grab, purchasers paid for it largely in scrip that had depreciated fifty percent or more from its face value.

Tax collectors and assessors, sheriffs and magistrates, and more than one governor, it was alleged, traded in state and foreclosed land, county bonds, and the ever-present scrip of many varieties. During eight years of Reconstruction following 1866, the state's debt rose by 900 percent.

Nearly evenly divided along political lines, Floridians sometimes supported Republican goals at the state level, while remaining solidly Democratic at the local level. This created a situation in which the most desirable political plums were likely to be up for grabs for the person who could buy or forge the most ballots.

The once-desolate peninsula was beginning to be eyed with interest by persons at a distance. Eli Thayer, a notable—or notorious—promoter of ambitious schemes that included "vast wagon trains bound for Kansas," drew up plans to establish in Florida a string of towns built especially for "soldier-colonists." Thayer's "model communities" never got off the drawing board, but he and others were sure that they glimpsed the glitter of gold in the sand of Florida.

Everything depended upon the prompt withdrawal of all Federal troops, would-be developers insisted. They watched with dread as military units stationed on the peninsula operated as usual, while troops were being withdrawn from other former Confederate states.

By 1875, according to John Wallace, it was clear that elections of the following year would be crucial. Hence the veteran lawmaker decried the four days of tumult at the Republican state convention in 1876. To make things worse, a rump group of "Reform" Republicans insisted upon holding a convention of their own. Like Democrats, members of both factions realized that the black vote was likely to be crucial.

"From the issuance of the call for the convention until and during its riotous sessions," wrote John Wallace, "whiskey was the strongest argument used to demoralize the colored people, with now and then a little money thrown in to keep up the hired loafers, who did nothing but follow up white carpetbag ballot-box stuffers and halloo themselves hoarse for the Republican candidate."

Whiskey, a little money, ballot box stuffers, and newly enfranchised black voters made a volatile and explosive combination. Yet, concluded John Wallace, these were the factors that would determine the future of his adopted state. "We've had a long struggle," he said many times, "and it is not over yet. But we have survived, and the person who makes it through struggle is always stronger at the end than at the beginning."

16

"As Florida Goes, So Goes the Nation"

Late in the evening of November 7, 1876, Gen. Dan Sickles was on his way home from the theater when he stopped at Republican headquarters in New York City. To his surprise, the place was deserted, and Democratic supporters of Samuel J. Tilden were claiming victory in the presidential election. The Republican national chairman had even gone home.

Sickles, who had lost a leg at Gettysburg, exploded when told that Zach Chandler had left word not to be disturbed. "He can go to bed if he wishes," snorted the fiery military leader. "But those of us who are men, have only begun to fight."

Supported by Gen. Chester A. Arthur, not yet widely regarded as a presidential hopeful, Sickles demanded details of what seemed to be a Republican loss. Tilden had a clear popular majority, he was told, but the electoral college was still in doubt. Three southern states were in turmoil. Using Chandler's name without authorization, Sickles fired off telegrams to Republican governors of these vital states.

By morning, many headlines proclaimed a Democratic victory. "Tilden Is Elected," said the New York Sun. In Chicago the Tribune lamented that "Tilden, Tammany, and the Solid South Are to Rule the Nation." New York's Herald exulted that the election produced "Complete Democratic Victory."

Looking at the early returns, managing editor John C. Reid of the New York Times had noticed that Florida,

Though Republicans controlled military forces of occupation, Democrats were accused of "bayonet rule." [LIBRARY OF CONGRESS]

South Carolina, and Louisiana remained under Republican control. That offered a ray of hope, he insisted. So his newspaper's headlines proclaimed, "Results Still Uncertain—A Solid South, Except Louisiana, Florida, and South Carolina."

Keenly sensitive to possibilities envisioned by General Sickles the previous evening, Reid hurried to Republican party headquarters. At his insistence, Zach Chandler dispatched identical telegrams to Republican governors of the crucial states: "Hayes is elected if we have carried South Carolina, Florida, and Louisiana. Can you hold your state? Answer immediately."

By the time Reid returned to his office, subordinates had made plans for page one of the issue of November 9. It declared, "Hayes has 185 electoral votes and is elected."

While that issue of the *Times* was being prepared,

prominent Republicans were making plans to go to Florida. Senator John Sherman of Ohio may have organized the group that included Rep. James Garfield of Ohio, Sen. John Kasson of Iowa, Gen. Lew Wallace, and Gen. Francis Barlow.

Before this contingent of dignitaries reached their destination, President U. S. Grant entered the fray. In a special order, he directed Gen. William T. Sherman to prepare to send more troops into Florida and Louisiana if it appeared that boards of canvassers would be threatened.

Canvassers were empowered to investigate charges of fraud and to certify the final tabulation of votes. In Florida the board was made up of three men: Secretary of State Samuel B. McLin, who had deserted from the Confederate army; Dr. C. A. Cowgill of Delaware, a Union veteran; and Attorney General William A. Cocke of Virginia. Cocke was the sole Democrat on the all-important board.

Before the board of canvassers was formally organized, charges and countercharges began accumulating. Escambia County Democrats were said to have voted at Pen-

Voter intimidation by Democratic hoodlums, as depicted by cartoonist A. B. Frost of New York. [NEW YORK PUBLIC LIBRARY]

sacola, then a second time at Bluff Springs and a third time at Perdido. In Jackson and other counties, forged ballots were said to have been prevalent. Wily Democrats allegedly printed ballots with the Republican insignia displayed prominently to catch the eyes of illiterate black voters. These "galvanized ballots" carried names of Democratic candidates below the Republican insignia and were said to have gotten into ballot boxes even in Leon County.

Election results announced by precincts gave the Democrats a slim majority. It appeared that they had swept the field, winning in the national and in most state contests. Still, Democrats announced plans to challenge results in ten counties; Republicans responded by contesting twenty-seven counties.

Facing the legal deadline imposed for the tabulation of electoral college votes for the presidency, Floridians of every political persuasion threw themselves into the fight. Everywhere there was talk of resuming the Civil War.

Canvassers, forming the official board in which one Democrat faced two Republicans on every issue, admitted, "It appears that Manatee County went ten to one for Tilden." Yet they threw out the entire vote of the county.

When the legal deadline for certification of electoral votes was reached, three sets of documents went to Washington. One of them was signed by Gov. Marcellus L. Stearns. A second was signed by the governor-elect, George F. Drew. William A. Cocke, minority member of the board of canvassers, submitted a third certificate that he signed in his role as Attorney-general of Florida.

Before these controversial certificates reached their destination, old Washington hands who seldom agreed on any issue had come to the verdict that "as Florida goes, so goes the nation."

In the nation's capital, Democrats claimed Florida and the White House. After all, the popular vote had shown that 262,292 citizens preferred Democrat Samuel Tilden over Republican Rutherford B. Hayes.

But the presidency is awarded by members of the electoral college, not by voters at the polls. With an impasse developing at that level, Congress took one of its most extraordinary actions ever. A special electoral commission was established, with authority to settle Florida and other disputed states.

Learned counsels appeared before the commission to argue the case for both the Republicans and the Democrats of Florida. Members of both parties feared that if no decision was reached, Ulysses S. Grant would remain in office.

One of the fifteen members of the electoral commission was Congressman James Garfield of Ohio. He had spent much of his own time and, according to rumor, great numbers of Republican dollars in Florida. Garfield never wavered in his insistence that, in that state, Hayes had won fairly, though only by a margin of forty-five popular votes.

Democrats, using every delaying tactic possible, managed to prevent final action by the electoral commission until Inauguration Day was at hand. Finally, at 4:00 A.M. on March 2, 1877, a joint session of Congress was informed that "Rutherford B. Hayes of Ohio, having received 185 electoral votes to Tilden's 184, is duly elected President of the United States for four years"—commencing in just forty-eight hours.

Democrats reluctantly agreed to let Florida tip the White House toward Hayes. But in a secret deal made hours before the announcement, authorities had promised to withdraw all Federal troops from Key West, Jacksonville, and other places still under occupation.

With Reconstruction finally ended, Florida was ready to take her place among the other states as an equal. As for the enterprising Ohio congressman who helped to swing Florida into the Republican column, even admiring colleagues did not then realize that James Garfield was headed for the White House.

17

Governor Bloxham Negotiated America's Biggest Land Deal

Outwardly calm to the extent of appearing jovial, William D. Bloxham was up-tight inside. Steadily drumming upon the table of a Philadelphia restaurant, he suddenly turned to an aide seated beside him and blurted, "Let's forget about sailfish, and go for tarpon!"

With his verdict barely out of his mouth, the governor of Florida jumped to his feet and pumped the hand of the guest he had been expecting.

They ate leisurely, talking only about hunting and fishing. Bloxham waited for just the right opportunity, then he complimented his guest for having learned to distinguish the feather of a hen from the feather of a cock on his first turkey hunt.

Hamilton Disston, who had inherited a fortune as a result of his father's success in manufacturing saws, modestly admitted that, for a novice, he had been exceptionally lucky when hunting wild turkeys. On a first-name basis with the governor as a result of several visits, he repeated what he had often said before: "Bill, you have the best hunting and fishing in the country— maybe the whole world!"

Acting upon that cue, Florida's chief executive talked with enthusiasm about "the greatest sport any man ever indulged in, bar none—salt-water fishing for tarpon." As his enthralled guest listened, Bloxham offered him the use of a state-owned vessel on his next trip south.

Only when the wealthy investor had accepted the invitation to fish for tarpon did the governor turn to a second topic. "Somebody's going to pick up a fortune from the Everglades one of these days," he commented.

Disston asked for more details, although he knew a little about the large land grant to the state from the federal government. Back in 1850 Congress had conveyed nearly seventy million acres of "swamp and overflowed land" to states in which such tracts were located. Florida received by far the biggest part of it, about twenty million acres.

That action on the part of national lawmakers came during a period when they were making a concerted effort to solve the slavery problem. Abolitionists wanted slavery outlawed in newly settled regions while advocates of slavery saw the creation of additional slave states as their only hope for maintaining the delicate balance in Congress.

As chief executive for sixteen months, feisty ex-soldier Zachary Taylor had blocked all proposals for territorial expansion of the United States or relinquishment of federally owned tracts within existing states. He wanted nothing to do with any enterprise that might foster the spread of slavery.

Millard Fillmore, his successor, was a self-taught ex-farmer and mill apprentice. When Henry Clay hammered out what he labeled as a lasting solution to the slavery problem, Fillmore gave his blessing to the Compromise of 1850.

Under its terms, to satisfy the South, Texas received ten million dollars to abandon its claims to the New Mexican territory, and a stricter federal law for the return of runaway slaves was enacted. To please the North, the slave trade was abolished in the District of Columbia, and California entered the Union without slavery. The territories of New Mexico and Utah were organized, each to determine its own stance on slavery.

In the climate of optimism created by passage of the compromise, Congress approved the Swamp Land Act on September 28, 1850. It was the fulfillment of a dream held by Floridians since their region was admitted to the Union.

However, legal and financial problems and the Civil

War had prevented Florida from doing anything with her bonanza. A special Internal Improvement Fund, created to oversee development and sale of state land, became hopelessly in debt.

Trustees of the state fund entered in their minutes such items as: newspaper ad, $5; telegrams, $3.88; monthly expenses of timber agent, $11.50.

Land offices had been opened in principal eastern cities, but even at fifty cents an acre there were few buyers. By 1880 the future of the state hung in the balance; only a really big land deal offered hope of a bail-out for debt-plagued Florida state agencies.

When energetic and personable William D. Bloxham became governor on January 4, 1881, he took it upon himself to clean up the state's financial mess. That is why he made his trip to Philadelphia to see Hamilton Disston, with whom he had become acquainted during the years in which the industrialist came to Florida to hunt and fish.

On the day of their momentous meeting, the president of the Keystone Saw, Tool, Steel, and File Works nodded interest when his friend mentioned the Everglades. Although considered worthless then, the immense region could be rich farming and cattle-raising country if someone with imagination and money drained it.

A general agreement was reached in a matter of hours and a detailed contract was signed on February 26. Under its terms, Disston and associates agreed "to drain and reclaim at their own expense and charge, all the overflowed lands south of specified boundaries."

Technically, it was a reclamation project rather than a conventional land purchase, but the deal required Florida to transfer to Disston four million acres of state-owned land. Thus, at age thirty-seven, Disston became the largest individual land owner in the United States. By December 31, 1881, the state was to be paid one million dollars in no more than four installments.

That contract meant that a nearly bankrupt state could avert disaster. And for Disston and associates, the biggest private land deal on record meant that they gained a tract almost twice as large as Connecticut, for twenty-five cents an acre.

A first payment of five hundred thousand dollars was made in May. Both the Tampa *Tribune* and the Fernandina *Mirror* criticized the sale, but the Apalachicola *Tribune* demanded to know who among the "growlers" would have paid two cents an acre for the vast tract.

The legal transfer of title, often involving two hundred thousand or more acres in a single deed, proceeded during the summer. Before cool weather reached Jacksonville, Disston sold two million acres to Sir Edward Reed of England.

The Philadelphia entrepreneur already had made plans to drain, clear, and develop the remaining two million acres. His engineers actually completed about ten miles of drainage canals. Disston City, not far from present-day

President Millard Fillmore assented to the Compromise of 1850 and the Swamp Land Act. [LIBRARY OF CONGRESS]

Gulfport, was platted into five- and ten-acre tracts, and an extensive advertising campaign was launched in northern cities.

Disston pumped money into projects aimed at fostering the production of sugar cane, rice, fruit, vegetables, and cattle. Kissimmee grew from a bedraggled cow town into what Disston's sale agents—not dimly dreaming of what lay in the faraway future—labeled "a magic city." A few English settlers took up tracts in the region bought by Reed and talked enthusiastically of "restoring this great region to its British heritage."

Side effects were dramatic.

Not only was the state and its agencies suddenly solvent, but Disston money spurred a burst of railroad construction. During 1881–82 more miles of track were completed than during the entire previous history of the peninsula. Florida's tax base doubled by 1885, and Bloxham rejoiced that the state had "no floating debt, and cash in the treasury."

But development plans of Disston and of Sir Edward Reed quickly soured. Colonists came in dribbles, not in droves; and few stayed for any length of time. Homesteaders and squatters caused constant legal problems. The cost of producing sugar proved greater than the market price, and drainage turned out to be far more complex and costly than promoters had imagined.

Then came the Panic of 1893. When Hamilton Disston died suddenly, his heavily mortgaged holdings were soon liquidated. Reed lost out, too. Measured by the standards of the time, both men suffered colossal losses.

Florida, however, proved to be the big winner. Boosted into solvency, the state won the favorable attention of Henry B. Plant, Henry M. Flagler, and other promoters from the north. In spite of boom-and-bust cycles, Florida was never again halted in her progress. The sale of swamp land in a colossal deal that today would be bitterly contested by environmentalists bailed out the state when many observers had gone on record as believing it would "go under, and stay under."

18

Florida's "Founder" Started with Nine Cents

"Now I can die happy; my dream is fulfilled!"

Eighty-two-year-old Henry Morrison Flagler acknowledged the applause of well-wishers gathered at the Key West railroad station. Then he spoke briefly of the fulfillment of his dream: a railroad stretching the entire length of Florida from the Georgia line to the Gulf of Mexico.

Flagler did not tell his listeners on January 22, 1912, that in an era when steak was selling for fifteen cents a pound, he had poured at least twenty million dollars into the last 156 miles of the Florida East Coast Railroad. More than three thousand men worked seven years to link Key West with Miami, with viaducts and bridges accounting for half the total mileage.

More than any other individual, Flagler deserves to be revered as "Florida's founder," modern Florida, that is. He first saw the Sunshine State at age fifty-three, when he spent a belated honeymoon in St. Augustine. It had taken ninety hours of travel to arrive in Jacksonville from New York City and another full day to reach his destination.

The charming oldest city in America, with a population of just about two thousand people, captivated Henry M. Flagler and his bride.

"This really would be a great place for winter visitors," he reputedly mused one day early in 1884, "if only there were decent facilities. One good hotel would make a world of difference."

Back in Florida two years later, the man who was a

The Ponce de Leon Hotel, St. Augustine, later served to house Flagler College. [THE HENRY MORRISON FLAGLER MUSEUM]

native of a village near Canandaigua, New York, found that New England businessmen had erected the San Marco Hotel in St. Augustine. Traveling in their private railroad car, "The Rambler," the Flaglers made the trip to Jacksonville, this time—in just two days.

"Got to have hotels to accommodate winter visitors," Flagler concluded. Almost as an afterthought he confided to his wife, "Hotels won't do much, without railroads."

Meditating upon the hotel/railroad combination, the New Yorker took part in St. Augustine's celebration of the landing of Ponce de León 373 years earlier. "That would make a great name for a really splendid hotel," he confided to his wife.

Already many times a millionaire as a result of an early partnership with John D. Rockefeller and a major role in founding the Standard Oil Company, Flagler poured 2.5 million dollars into the Ponce de León Hotel in St. Augustine. When it opened on January 10, 1888, oldtimers in Florida admitted, "This state has never seen anything like the Ponce."

A string of other luxury hotels followed: the Alcazar in St. Augustine, the Ormond in Ormond, and, much later, the Royal Poinciana and the Breakers at Palm Beach, and the Royal Palm at Miami.

Flagler expected to make money, but to intimates he confessed that he already had more than he would ever spend. He was more interested in seeing "this vast sun-drenched wilderness made into a vacation mecca" than in amassing additional millions.

Early in the expansion of his chain of hotels, the New Yorker came back to an earlier conclusion: no matter how delightful hotels in Florida might be, they would be nearly empty unless served by good railroads.

That started his acquisition and combining of short rail lines, later extending new tracks deeper into the Florida peninsula. Because it meant that people from all of the North could travel comfortably to any point in Florida, completion of the line from Miami to Key West really was the culmination of a grand goal conceived nearly thirty years earlier.

At least one modern biographer has called Henry M. Flagler a "visionary robber baron." There is little doubt that the estimated sixty million dollars he poured into Florida enterprises made more millions for him. He clearly was a visionary, but he was not a robber baron, at least not in Florida.

Flagler gave free seed and cuttings to orange growers. The son of a Presbyterian minister, he built Presbyterian, Methodist, and Baptist churches and paid for the renova-tion of St. Augustine's Catholic cathedral. Throughout his adopted state, "the Flagler impact" from generous gifts, often anonymous, can be seen in public buildings and municipal facilities.

In no other state has a single person had an influence comparable to that of Henry M. Flagler upon Florida. That impact is dramatized by a tour guide's comment: "Mr. Flagler was a high school dropout who left home at age fourteen with nine cents in his pocket."

His elegantly furnished Whitehall mansion, built in Palm Beach at a cost of four million dollars, is now a mu-seum. Open to the public—complete with Mr. Flagler's re-stored private railroad car—it invites a minimum of one hour of browsing and meditating. For more information, write to the museum on Cocoanut Row or telephone (407) 655-2833.

19

Sixty-foot Bamboo Lured Thomas A. Edison to the Caloosahatchee

Fort Myers
July 18 & Oct. 18, 1885

Studying plans for our Floridian bower, within that charmed zone of beauty where wafted from the table lands of the Orinoco and the dark Carib Sea, perfumed zephyrs forever kiss the gorgeous florae.

We will erect two dwellings on the riverfront, and place the laboratory and dwellings for workmen on the other side of the street.

Thomas A. Edison

Scientist Thomas A. Edison, already world famous for his inventions of the electric light and the phonograph, praised Florida in his diary and letters. Some of his writing literally sang its way across the pages.

Like Hamilton Disston, Edison was drawn south by the promise of good hunting and fishing. With colleague Ezra Gilliland—like Edison, a former telegrapher—he reached St. Augustine from New Orleans in the middle of winter.

They crossed the peninsula on a rickety train that required two days for the 125-mile trip. On the Gulf coast, someone casually said that at Fort Myers bamboo grew sixty feet tall.

Edison was instantly ready to see this for himself. Bamboo was essential for the production of his incandescent lamps. He had tried thousands of organic materials and found nothing that glowed so brightly for so long as did strips of bamboo. At the moment, his agents were combing the jungles of South America and the Orient in search

*Thomas Edison after five days of continuous work on his pho-
nograph.*

of just the right bamboo for making filaments. Perhaps
this wonderful growth at the remote Florida village would
be precisely what he sought!

Earlier envisioned by Hamilton Disston as the gateway
to his Everglades empire, Fort Myers had a population of
fifty or so people. Alligators, flamingos, and deer
abounded, along with towering bamboo and orange trees
at least twenty-five feet tall.

Thomas Edison, age thirty-eight, was instantly enam-
ored with the place. When he began poking around, asking the value of land, the tiny Fort Myers *Press* newspaper—just launched—informed readers that "Thomas
A. Edison, the electrician, is visiting here."

He found a fourteen-acre tract with four hundred feet of
frontage on the river that was as beautiful as its name.
Soon he put down earnest money to bind an option for
purchase of the place for $2,750. Already, in his imagina-
tion he could see it graced with a rambling home that he
intended to call Seminole Lodge.

Lumber would be cut in Maine, where it would be

formed into prefabricated sections and shipped from Boston, he decided. There was no other way to build the dwelling he wanted in the primitive place he had selected for his winter home. A widower for a year, Edison soon brought his second bride to the yet uncompleted Seminole Lodge.

Within days the daughter of an Akron, Ohio, philanthropist developed what became a lifelong passion for the good life in Fort Myers.

Encouraged by her, Edison gave the completion of his laboratory priority over their living quarters in Seminole Lodge. "This place is good for you," his bride frequently reminded him. "You were far from well when you first arrived—but the sunshine and the clear air soon restored you to health. You ought to spend as little time as possible in the north."

Edison heeded her advice. For fifty years Seminole Lodge was the place he most loved to be. As he had expected, he made good use of Florida bamboo, until Europeans discovered how to pulverize cotton so that it could be squirted out to form a filament far more uniform than bamboo strips.

In Fort Myers he worked on his motion picture camera, the fluoroscope, which led to fluorescent lights, the alkaline storage battery, the disc phonograph, talking motion pictures, and—above all—rubber from a native American source.

Rubber became scarce and expensive during World War I. Nearly a decade later the supply again dried up and the price rose when a British monopoly restricted shipment of latex from the Orient. Henry Ford, whose plantation was separated from Seminole Lodge only by a fence, became alarmed. If he could not get sufficient rubber at a satisfactory price, he would have to cut production of Model-T Fords.

Harvey Firestone agreed that they—and the nation—faced a crisis. Hence they turned to their mutual friend—Edison—and asked him to put everything else aside and find a domestic source of rubber for them.

Climate made the region adjoining Seminole Lodge just right to grow and test so many plants that Mrs. Edison came close to complaining. "Everything turned to rubber," she later said. "We talked rubber, thought rubber, and dreamed rubber; Mr. Edison wouldn't let us do anything else."

With an initial one hundred thousand dollars each from Ford and Firestone, the great inventor collected and tested at least 3,200 wild plants during twelve months. More money was poured into research, making it possible for fourteen thousand plants to be tested by the end of the second year. At least six hundred had sap that included rubber-like components. Although honeysuckle and milkweed seemed to offer special promise, Edison concluded that goldenrod was the solution to America's crucial need for rubber.

"Give me five years," he promised Henry Ford, "and the United States will have a rubber crop."

Selective crossbreeding produced splendid fourteen-foot stalks of goldenrod, yielding nearly twelve percent

The Edison winter home in Fort Myers was prefabricated from the inventor's own drawings.

latex. Hence Henry Ford bought eight thousand acres in Georgia for use as a goldenrod plantation.

Clearly, the man at Seminole Lodge was on the verge of success with rubber from goldenrod. Then came word that German scientists had developed a new chemical process. Now petroleum derivations could be converted into synthetic rubber with some properties superior to those of natural rubber.

Harvey Firestone had already received a batch of goldenrod latex from Florida. So he used it to make a set of tires for Edison's Model-A Ford touring car.

The collapse of the rubber empire as it was about to be launched did not diminish the stature of Thomas A. Edison. More than a century after he became a Floridian by choice, he still stands above every other inventor of the Western world.

After his death in 1931, Mina Miller Edison gave Seminole Lodge and the surrounding estate to Fort Myers as a memorial to her late husband. Today the museum/laboratory/botanical gardens is one of the "must visit" sites of Florida's west coast. Closed only on Thanksgiving and Christmas, the shrine packed with memorabilia is surrounded by native flowering plants and trees and also the South American rain tree, the sausage tree from Africa, an immense fig from Australia (potentially a source of rubber), and the strange dynamite tree. When ripe, the tomatolike seed pods of the thorn-covered tree explode violently, spewing seeds as far as four hundred feet.

Plan to spend half a day at the Thomas A. Edison Home and surrounding gardens, preferably in March or early April when the products of the inventor's mind and hands are made even more dramatic by the natural background. That is when the cochlospermum displays its double yellow flowers, the towering hibiscus alata is a blaze of crimson, African tulips and wild orchids are at their peak, and the exotic perfume of the frangipani from Mexico scents the breeze.

For full information, address Edison Winter Home, 2350 McGregor Boulevard, Fort Myers, FL 33901; telephone (813) 267-2533.

20

At Cocoanut Grove, Alexander Graham Bell's Tongue Was Well Oiled

Florida sunshine is the world's finest lubricant. When it oils up a fellow's tongue, he'll tell you everything he knows—and a whole lot that he doesn't know.
—Late nineteenth-century folk saying

In Miami's Cocoanut Grove suburb, the man who invented the telephone soaked up the sunshine. On many days his daughter put him in a wheelchair, pushed him to a spot that was radiantly bright but comfortably cool and left him there for hours contentedly watching birds dart and swirl overhead.

That is where the president of a group of realtors saw him day after day. With the inventor's seventy-fifth birthday close at hand, his new acquaintance asked him to speak at the weekly luncheon of the realty board.

"You don't have to have a prepared speech," he urged. "Just talk to us about some of your experiences."

Bell, who seldom accepted invitations of any sort, said he thought he would enjoy taking part in the meeting. At first he considered talking about his spacious home in Nova Scotia and nearby Beinn Breach Mountain, where he expected to be buried.

Then he changed his mind. After all, the residents of Cocoanut Grove were "home folks" to him. For years he had spent as many months as possible there each season.

"Perhaps you have read about my good fortune at the Centennial Exposition," tradition asserts he told realtors when he began speaking. "Even if you know about it, I hope I can add something fresh.

107

"At that time, I was planning to resume my teaching of the deaf. I had very little money and didn't intend to waste any of it on a trip to Philadelphia. But I consented to go to the station to see one of my pupils off; she badly wanted to help celebrate our nation's one hundredth birthday."

At the station, nineteen-year-old Mabel Hubbard signaled her teacher that she expected him to go with her. On impulse, Bell jumped aboard the train without baggage or ticket.

To his surprise, he found himself a minor celebrity in Philadelphia. Officials of the exposition insisted that he give a public demonstration of his telephone on a Sunday afternoon.

"It was very hot—not at all like Cocoanut Grove," Bell remembered. "All of the judges were tired, and I was sure that they would not go through with the demonstration."

Suddenly an aide-surrounded dignitary stepped to Bell's side. Dom Pedro, emperor of Brazil, pumped the hand of the inventor and said he had heard much about him. "You must proceed with your demonstration," he insisted.

A wire had already been strung around the room, with an instrument attached to each end. Youthful Alexander Graham Bell picked up the transmitter and pointed Dom Pedro to the receiver. As soon as the emperor placed the receiver to his ear, he exclaimed, "My God! It really *does* talk!"

Chuckling as he recalled events that took place nearly half a century earlier, Bell noted that the sudden appearance of the emperor "turned a wash-out into a hullabaloo that lasted until 10:00 P.M."

An enthralled listener signaled, caught the speaker's attention, and inquired, "What kind of telephone do you use in your laboratory, Mr. Bell—a wall model, or a desk model?"

Alexander Graham Bell hesitated momentarily. Eyes suddenly twinkling, he replied, "Neither. I don't want a telephone anywhere close to the place where I work or study!"

Alexander Graham Bell, calling Chicago from New York in 1892. [AMERICAN TELEPHONE AND TELEGRAPH COMPANY]

Newspapers around the world published accounts of the Cocoanut Grove realty board's luncheon. Responding to questions from a reporter for a Miami newspaper, Bell confessed, "There is no telephone in the residence of my daughter, Mrs. Fairchild, either."

Red-faced subordinates at the famous laboratory established by Alexander Graham Bell admitted they had been sitting on a secret for twenty years. The man who created the telephone had very little use for his own invention. Occasionally he consented to make ceremonial calls for the sake of photographers, but in private life he managed very well without a telephone at his elbow.

Oral tradition in the Miami region asserts that in later conversations with realtors Bell revealed that he had become bored with the telephone once eight thousand patents had been developed as a result of his initial one. "Privacy is the real reason I do not have a telephone in my workplace," he admitted. "I cannot afford the luxury of frequent interruptions; they would cost me too much damage to my thought processes."

The better to explain what he meant, Bell resorted to metaphor and compared an idea-filled mind with a tub of water. When ideas were forming in his mind, he said, they gradually came together and "quieted down."

When an invention was close to the patent stage or an idea was nearly completed, the inventor said his mind was like a tub of water whose surface was as smooth as glass. Any kind of interruption, he insisted, came in much the same way as a brick dropped into a tub of water. "Splash! Splash! Suddenly the whole surface of the tub of water is turbulent and agitated."

Since a disturbed idea is an idea gone, perhaps forever, Bell said, "When I am thinking, I want no one to disturb me for any reason. Messages can wait; ideas cannot."

Corporations that profited from Alexander Bell's invention had for years managed to keep his attitude toward it from becoming public knowledge. Even thick biographies that emphasize his nocturnal habits and liking for solitude seldom mention his attitude toward his invention that changed the world.

Except in newspapers of March 1922, it is all but impossible to find even brief published references to the sudden admission made by the inventor when his tongue was well oiled with Florida sunshine.

21

For Half a Century Estero Was the Center of the Universe

"We shall build a 'Wonder City,' a place of racial peace and harmony where six to ten million persons of all races will live and work together in total love," promised Cyrus R. Teed.

His Chicago audience applauded so wildly that the speaker departed from his plan of secrecy. "We shall call our great city New Jerusalem," he confided. Then he leaned forward and in a stage whisper informed ecstatic listeners, "By careful mathematical calculations, New Jerusalem will be located at the precise center of the universe."

Only his chief aides knew that Teed had traveled throughout Florida late in 1893. At Estero, a few miles south of Fort Myers, he accepted from Gustav Damkoehler a gift of three hundred acres of fertile land. With money contributed by his faithful followers, he secured options on an additional one thousand acres. Clearly, that was the unannounced site of the vast utopian city he planned to build.

Teed was a native of New York State who had studied medicine briefly and claimed to have entered the U.S. Army medical corps in 1860 at age twenty-one. In uniform, he soon experienced what today would be called battle fatigue. While recuperating, he received a series of life-changing revelations.

Meditating upon these mystical experiences, the young physician developed a comprehensive doctrine of "cellular cosmogony." According to it, all existing theories about the earth and the universe were erroneous.

By the time he was back in civilian life, Dr. Teed had decided to give up medicine to spread the gospel of cellular cosmogony. "You have been told that the earth is a solid sphere," he said to anyone who would listen. "My revelations have shown that it is not solid. Instead, it is a hollow ball about seven thousand miles in diameter. The sun, the moon, and the stars are near the middle of the sphere, while the continents and oceans are spread out around its inner surface."

For twenty years after the end of the Civil War, Dr. Teed was the subject of an occasional newspaper story. Having proclaimed himself to be Cyrus, the Messenger, he organized followers into the Society Arch Triumphant. Before being admitted to full membership and assigned a place in the Chicago headquarters of the society, a convert was required to sever all family ties, surrender all belongings, and take a vow of perpetual celibacy.

Claiming to have four thousand followers, Cyrus received another revelation ordering him to change his name to the Hebrew equivalent of Cyrus: Koresh. This means, he said, "the great leader at the core of the universe." He then changed the name of his sect to Koreshan Unity.

"Construction of the city will provide for a number of different elevations of streets," one of his publications promised. That plan would put heavy team traffic on the bottom elevation, light driving above it, with pedestrians and railroads being assigned to other levels.

Generations ahead of city planners, his multilevel passageways were touted as making travel in New Jerusalem as rapid and as effortless as though one were in a village, rather than in the world's largest metropolis.

New Jerusalem was to be constructed by volunteer labor "without the use of so-called money." Work began before anyone—even Teed—had adopted the label "environmentalist." Yet the city plan given to Koresh by illumination stressed that there would be no pollution in it.

"There will be no dumping of sewage into the streams,

bay, or Gulf. A movable and continuous earth closet will carry the debris and *offal* of the city to a place thirty or more miles distant, where it will be transformed into fertilizer. There will be no smudge or smoke."

A construction crew reached Estero some time in February or March 1894, but nearly a decade passed before Unity headquarters was moved from Chicago to Florida. By then, New Jerusalem boasted separate dormitories for men and women, a dining hall, a saw mill, and numerous barns and outbuildings.

Once the headquarters of the sect reached the center of the universe, acquisition of land proceeded rapidly. Bowing briefly to local political pressure, residents held a town meeting late in 1904 and voted to incorporate. With more than 6,000 acres already owned by Koreshan Unity, or under lease, it was announced that New Jerusalem was 110 square miles in size.

"When Koresh appeared before his followers in order to address them, his restless brown eyes glowed like embers," according to a contemporary account. "A few words from his mouth had a mesmerizing influence over those who listened—especially younger members of the

Cyrus R. Teed [FLORIDA DEPARTMENT OF ARCHIVES AND HISTORY]

female persuasion."

Missionaries who fanned out from New Jerusalem preached the gospel of the hollow earth. They invited all who would listen to give up worldly concerns and gain enlightenment in a series of progressive steps that would bring them to full membership in Koreshan Unity.

However, few natives of Lee County paid any attention to the newcomers. Occasionally the Fort Myers *Press* pointed out that the Estero colony comprised the largest band of people from the Northeast and Midwest yet to congregate at one place in Florida.

Nevertheless, editors of national newspapers began to pay attention when it was learned that New Jerusalem had been platted to accommodate a minimum of eight million residents, with four-hundred-foot streets for multilevel transportation. Not all were convinced. A 1907 editorial in the Tallahassee *Sun* declared that the founder of the city "is not the first rascal who has made religion a cloak for his designs against the property and personal liberty of others. But he is the only one now allowed to do business in Florida."

Koresh, or Cyrus R. Teed as some newspapers still insisted upon calling him, reacted with a stinging attack upon the press in general and the Tallahassee *Sun* in particular. However, with momentum building toward a spectacular confrontation, the builder of New Jerusalem died suddenly on December 22, 1908.

All activity in the city came to a halt with Koresh's death. After four days of mourning, followers buried him at the tip of Estero Island. Membership—never really large—soon began to shrink. Half a century after their utopian city was laid out, the handful of remaining members of Koresh Unity disbanded.

Located just off interstate highway 75, Koreshan State Historic Site on the banks of the Estero River affords a look at the restored utopian community. Allow at least an hour for a tour of the buildings and grounds said to mark the center of the universe. For more information call (813) 992-0311.

22

Julia Tuttle Sent Orange Blossoms to Flagler

At St. Augustine on the night before Christmas 1894, it was apparent that Henry M. Flagler's dreams for Florida might well prove to be empty. The thermometer had dropped to about eighteen degrees, and long before word began trickling to his headquarters, the hotel and railroad builder knew that most of the state's citrus and vegetable crops were destroyed.

Flagler acted with characteristic speed. Aides were assigned to stricken areas, told to get there by the fastest possible means, and immediately to begin giving assistance to farmers, ranchers, and citrus growers. Tradition has it that Flagler was at the bank before it opened on December 26 to withdraw one hundred thousand dollars in cash and distribute it among his messengers.

Although the winter vegetable market was strong and growing rapidly, the citrus industry remained the dominant money producer of Florida. While the loss of an entire crop was bad enough, even worse, Flagler insisted, was the probability that many in the north would lose confidence in the ability of his adopted state to produce without interruption.

As Henry M. Flagler paced the floor, firing off telegrams and waiting for firm assessments of damage, a messenger appeared. "This is for Mr. Flagler, personally," he told the aide who stepped forward.

There was momentary uncertainty, during which the messenger remained unyielding. He would not deliver his package to anyone other than the man to whom it was

Julia Tuttle [FLORIDA DEPARTMENT OF ARCHIVES AND HISTORY]

consigned. When Flagler finally came into the room, to his astonishment he was handed a bundle of orange blossoms.

"They come from Mrs. Julia Tuttle at Biscayne," said the messenger. "She again invites you to visit her at Fort Dallas and to inspect fields and groves without frost damage."

Half a dozen stories circulate about the events that followed Julia Tuttle's gift. One of them, perhaps the most believable, has the railroad magnate and chief aide James Ingraham boarding a launch and heading south without waiting to pack their belongings. After transferring to a mule-drawn wagon at New River, they reached Fort Dallas muddy and bedraggled where Julia Tuttle greeted them at the gate.

"We have corresponded often, but now I am here in person," said John D. Rockefeller's business partner. "I am Henry Flagler, and these must be the shores of paradise itself!"

According to that account, Flagler and Mrs. Tuttle talked for less than an hour, then drew up a tentative agreement for development of the area surrounding Fort Dallas.

Born in Ohio to a mother who had taught in the Indian

school at Tallahassee, Julia Tuttle's ties with Florida were strong. After her marriage, her parents moved to the peninsula, where she often visited them. When Frederick Tuttle died of tuberculosis in 1886, his widow decided to take her two children where they would be unlikely to die of their father's illness.

A quick look at California was enough; after her second day in the state, she decided she preferred south Florida. Long-abandoned Fort Dallas looked as though it could be repaired and used as a residence, so she bought the post once used by soldiers, with 644 surrounding acres.

Soon after having become a permanent resident of Florida in November 1891, Julia Tuttle began badgering Henry M. Flagler. Time after time, she tried to persuade him to visit her region. If he would only come, she insisted, he would decide to extend his railroad to Biscayne Bay.

Usually polite Flagler became impatient at the widow's continued pleas. His replies to her letters became increasingly terse, even abrupt. Yes, he was well aware she was willing to deed half of her land to him. No, he did not intend to extend his rail line below Lake Worth. Yes, he really was planning to dig a great canal, by means of

The Miami railroad station, about 1900. [FLORIDA DEPARTMENT OF ARCHIVES AND HISTORY]

which Lake Worth would be linked with Biscayne by water. No, he would not use barges on the canal; it would become an important route for steamers.

Rebuffed many times, Julia Tuttle persevered. And her orange blossoms, delivered during the panic of the great freeze of 1894–95, produced results. No other persuasion was needed. Flagler could see that the great tract of land between the southern tip of the Everglades and the Atlantic Ocean was perhaps the most protected place in all Florida. At least forty miles long, it offered shelter from even the severest winter weather.

The developer and the widow entered into a formal contract in February 1895. She retained Fort Dallas and thirteen surrounding acres. One hundred acres of her land was designated as the site for a railroad terminal, sidings, and a hotel.

More than five hundred acres of undeveloped land remained. Julia Tuttle refused to cede her land in one big block, even though she had earlier promised to give Flagler half of it in return for bringing a railroad to the region. Instead, she divided the acreage into strips, then deeded alternate ones to Flagler, keeping the rest for herself.

Henry Morrison Flagler [THE HENRY MORRISON FLAGLER MUSEUM]

Once the deal was completed, Flagler swung into action. Soon the sleepy fishing village of Miami was incorporated. Gangs of laborers recruited throughout the state worked to build a water tower, lay out streets, and cut a channel deep enough to permit ocean-going steamers to make Miami a port of call. Flagler made plans to build what would be his finest hotel and pushed the promised extension of his railroad.

By the time the first locomotive reached the site of modern Miami in February 1896, Julia Tuttle was busy with her own enterprises. From a small herd of cows, she expanded to form the Fort Dallas Dairy, which won the contract to supply milk to all of Flagler's hotels. She bought stock in the Bank of Bay Biscayne, Miami's first bank, and became a director of it. With land values going up, she refused to part with any of the strips she retained in the arrangement with Flagler. Instead of selling, she bought land as rapidly as possible, even when she had to borrow to do so. Many guests from the north who attended the gala opening of Flagler's lemon-yellow Royal Palm Hotel were awed to learn that a nondescript-looking woman held title to much of the region.

To finance her dairy and other enterprises, at age forty-seven the widow needed forty thousand dollars. Her bank did not have that much cash to lend, so she persuaded Flagler to endorse her note issued by a New York bank. Then, in the backwash of the Panic of 1893, the directors of the New York bank sounded as though they might demand immediate payment in cash.

Desperate, Julia Tuttle reputedly turned to Flagler once more. This time she offered him her entire Miami holdings for eighty thousand dollars. Flagler is said to have responded that he already owned half of Miami and did not need the other half. Therefore, at her death in September 1898, half of Miami was inherited by her heirs.

At the time the will was probated, a keen observer noted that "The decedent, Mrs. Julia DeForest Sturdevant Tuttle, was a Biscayne resident for only seven years."

23

No More Fear of Spain!

"The city of Miami is helpless to defend herself. Refugees arriving daily from Cuba talk freely of a coming invasion. We must have help immediately."

Dispatched to President William McKinley in secret, that telegram was sent by the mayor of Miami early in March 1898. It did not bring engineers to build fortifications as citizens had hoped. Instead, McKinley gave instructions that Miami would become a garrison for troops.

Oldtimers relaxed when they learned that the fast-growing town would become a staging area for the expected invasion of Cuba. A few units from the thirty thousand-man U.S. Army, plus three or four companies of volunteers, began erecting a camp in April.

Late that month, however, panic gripped Miami and all of Florida. Rumor had it that Spanish Admiral Pascual Cervera was leading his fleet from the Cape Verde Islands toward an unknown target on the east coast of the United States. Once the report was pronouncd genuine, many newcomers to the land of Julia Tuttle and Henry Flagler hastened to return north.

During nineteen days of tension, some Miami residents tried to rig makeshift barriers that they hoped might protect their homes from Spanish bullets. Then it was learned that the enemy fleet had reached a Cuban seaport. For the first time since the destruction of the battleship *Maine*, Floridians began to feel secure.

The hull of the U.S.S. Maine *was launched at Brooklyn in 1890.*
[HARPER'S WEEKLY]

Strained relations between the United States and Spain in the late 1890s were made worse by a clamor for independence on the part of many Cubans. Tens of thousands of Americans felt it their patriotic duty to go to the aid of revolutionary forces on the island and, simultaneously, to give Spain a licking she would never forget.

President McKinley authorized the mission that took the U.S.S. *Maine* to Havana—into Spanish waters. The battleship was sent there, said the president, to protect American lives and property during the revolution that was sure to break out very soon.

Twenty-one days after her anchor was dropped, the *Maine* was ripped apart by a tremendous explosion that took the lives of approximately 264 crew members. Before an investigation could be launched, the newspaper empire of William Randolph Hearst began clamoring for war with Spain as retaliation for events on the night of February 15, 1898.

"Remember the *Maine!*" became a national battlecry. Congress authorized a three hundred percent increase in the size of the regular army and the creation of a volunteer force of two hundred thousand men. President McKinley asked lawmakers for a formal resolution to permit him to take steps to restore peace to Cuba.

In a joint resolution of April 20, Congress recognized the independence of Cuba, demanded the withdrawal of Spanish armed forces, and authorized the president to use any means necessary to implement congressional wishes.

America's navy, far stronger than the Spanish navy and a great deal better prepared for war than the U.S. Army, threw up a blockade around Cuba. Goaded into action, Spain declared war on April 24. One day later, the United States declared war upon Spain.

Even before the formal declaration of war, Americans knew that Florida would be the jumping-off place for the struggle in Cuba. On the peninsula few failed to realize that the coming military action would pump immense amounts of money into the local economy.

U.S. Army headquarters were established in Tampa, with Gen. William R. Shafter in command. Before reaching his post, he issued orders that led to expansion of the camps around Miami. Soon more than seven thousand men were spending their paychecks in the city that a few months earlier had been described as economically depressed.

So many volunteers flocked to Florida camps that it was difficult to house and to feed them. Everywhere, Americans of almost every persuasion were eager for the war. Assistant Secretary of the Navy Theodore Roosevelt resigned his post to become a lieutenant colonel in a cavalry unit headed for Cuba.

Key West became the headquarters of the American naval operation. Special excitement was created on May 26, when the battleship *Oregon* reached the Florida port after having steamed 14,760 miles from San Francisco. Her tremendous journey around Cape Horn added to growing American interest in building a canal across the Isthmus of Panama to cut weeks off voyages from one coast of the United States to the other.

A naval court of inquiry, established to investigate the

One-time Rough Rider
Theodore Roosevelt,
president of the United
States

explosion that sent the *Maine* to the bottom, reported, "A submarine mine" no doubt planted by Spaniards was clearly the culprit.

That hasty conclusion became highly suspect in later decades. The cause of the explosion has never been definitely proved. Today it is believed that Spain had nothing to do with it and that careless handling of ammunition, gun-cotton, or detonators—even coal dust in fuel bunkers—could have ignited to launch a chain reaction within the ship. But in 1898 no one wished to examine alternatives that might relieve Spain of culpability.

Military movement proceeded with such speed there was much confusion at Florida bases. When the time set for invasion by land forces was reached, it proved impossible to get horses aboard ships hardly big enough for the troops consigned to them. As a result, the animals remained in Florida, causing Teddy Roosevelt and his famous Rough Riders to charge up San Juan Hill on foot.

In spite of gaffes such as this, "the splendid little war" was a howling success for the United States—and for Florida. So much money poured into Miami that the city was able to open a telephone exchange before the end of 1898. Throughout the state, buildings erected for military purposes were converted into civilian uses. A few camps and installations were made permanent, notably the naval base at Key West.

Even more important than the big financial gains from the war was the assurance that—at last—Floridians need have no more fear of Spain. The war that lasted for only 105 days of combat resulted in Spain's loss of much of her centuries-old empire. Simultaneously, the United States became established—for the first time—as a world power. It gained new territories: Guam, the Philippines, and Puerto Rico. Accepting its "destiny" of imperialism, it annexed the Hawaiian Republic, previously a virtual protectorate. The U.S. Navy was now dominant in the Caribbean Sea, and long-dormant plans for building a trans-Isthmian canal were revived.

As for the victims of the *Maine* disaster, Spanish authorities initially offered to bury them in Cuba. That idea was indignantly rejected; these heroes would be buried only on American soil—at Arlington National Cemetery.

Time passed, and enthusiasm waned. As a result, visitors to the Key West Cemetery may see there a special memorial beneath which lie the bodies of those whose death in Havana touched off the Spanish-American War.

At 401 West Kennedy Boulevard in Tampa, Plant Hall of the University of Tampa occupies what was once the Tampa Bay Hotel. Because this historic structure was Theodore Roosevelt's headquarters during the Spanish-American War, it marks the site at which his rise to the presidency began. Today the south wing houses the Henry B. Plant Museum, for which visitors should allow one to two hours. For more information, call (813) 253-3333.

PART FOUR:

A Growing Mecca for Men and Women on the Creative Edge

With Florida lifted to new prominence by innovators such as Disston, Flagler, Edison, and Bell, the region attracted increasing numbers of creative persons. Simultaneously, natives of the peninsula that was becoming a tourist mecca gained recognition by their achievements.

Youthful educator Mary McLeod Bethune [Bethune-Cookman College]

24

Mary McLeod Bethune Started with Boundless Faith — Plus $1.50

"You told me that you'd like for me to be a trustee of a school," said James N. Gamble. Son of the founder of Procter and Gamble and a newcomer who was building a home at Daytona Beach, Gamble's voice and face revealed his bewilderment.

"I've been here nearly half an hour," he continued, "and I have seen nothing that looks like a school. Pray tell me, just where is this school?"

Mary McLeod Bethune, age twenty-nine, rose from the wobbly chair behind the wooden crate that served her as a desk. "That school is right here, Mr. Gamble," she fired back at him. "Right here—in my mind and in my soul!"

That exchange became the springboard for a torrent of words from the woman whose parents spent most of their lives in slavery. She spoke fervently of her dreams of a school for the education of black girls. She recalled her own childhood experiences and relived the magic moment when she discovered that black shapes printed upon paper can convey sounds and sights and colors and meanings.

Before the afternoon was over, Gamble had agreed to become chairman of a board of trustees. Four other men—Mayor E. L. Smith, a realtor, and two ministers—said they would serve as trustees. All had gathered in a small frame cottage on Palm Street at the urgent insistence of Mrs. Bethune.

Gamble immediately contacted his attorney, Bert Fish, and asked him to draw up a charter. When the document

Mary McLeod Bethune with President
Hamilton Holt of Rollins College, where she
became the nation's first black woman to receive a honorary degree from a southern college. [ROLLINS COLLEGE]

was completed and approved by the trustees, the Daytona
Literary and Industrial School for Training Negro Girls
was legally in existence.

Actually, the school had been born a few months earlier. While teaching in a missionary school at Palatka,
Mary McLeod Bethune envisioned an educational institution that would help to raise members of her race from
ignorance and poverty. Since it had to be located in the
South, she investigated sites in her native South Carolina,
as well as in Georgia and Alabama. Finally she selected

Daytona Beach as "just the right spot."

With her mind and spirit so full of the institution she foresaw, her immediate vision may have been defective. Hence she found no fault with a two-story frame building near the railroad when she learned that it might be for rent.

Three rooms downstairs and two rooms upstairs would serve nicely as living quarters for her family and school-rooms for future students, she concluded. A query to the owner brought dismaying news. The rent would be eleven dollars a month.

"I'll take it, just as soon as the railroad men you have in it can move out," said Mrs. Bethune. "Here," she continued, reaching into her pocket, "you can have a dollar and a half right now; I'll pay the rest by the end of the month."

Initially hesitant, the owner agreed to accept the only cash his new tenant had. She immediately began planning a return trip to Palatka to move furniture and bring along her husband and their five-year-old son. Before she could arrange transportation, however, she got word that their home had burned and nothing was saved from the flames.

"No need to go back to Palatka," she said to herself. "Might as well get busy, right here."

Merchants donated packing cases, one sturdy barrel, and a few wooden boxes. Once these were converted into makeshift chairs and desks, she was ready to go into the streets to solicit pupils, small girls whose mothers started to work very early in the morning and needed a place to leave their children.

On October 4, 1904, Anna, Ruth, Lena, Celeste, and Lucille assembled at the rented house, standing at the door, waiting awkwardly. Inside, Mrs. Bethune tapped a nickel-plated desk bell, strode to the door, and invited them, "Come in, girls. We've been expecting you. I hope you will be happy with us."

A few weeks spent prowling through trash dumps in search of things that could be salvaged served to convince the founder of the school that she would need help. Even the sweet potato pies she baked in the evening to sell every morning to men who had come to Daytona Beach to help build Henry M. Flagler's railroad did not yield enough profit to keep her dream alive.

Therefore she decided to recruit men who would serve as trustees and to make a five dollar down payment on a fifty-foot by one hundred-foot lot that she believed to be a suitable building site.

Once her 250-dollar real estate purchase was firm and her board of trustees was organized, she erected a hand-lettered sign that pointed to the empty lot purchased for the school.

Increasing numbers of Northerners were spending the winter at Daytona Beach. One of them, Pittsburgh music store proprietor C. C. Mellour, suggested that she dress her girls in uniform and give concerts at the hotels. Surprisingly, contributions from listeners piled up much faster than had profits from sweet potato pies.

A casual visitor, who watched small girls in a dress-making class struggle with a decrepit Singer sewing machine, wrote out a check for 250 dollars. On the following day he came back, this time with a brand new White sewing machine, a gift to the school.

"When I recovered from my daze," Mrs. Bethune often said in later years, "I suddenly realized that our new benefactor was Thomas H. White, head of the sewing machine company that was the chief competitor of the Singer Company."

For the educator, surprises started very early. On the five-acre farm at Mayesville, South Carolina, where she was reared, she could pick 250 pounds of cotton a day at age nine, but she did not know one letter of the alphabet from another. When northern Presbyterians opened a mission school five miles from the log cabin of her parents, they decided that Mary, the youngest girl among their seventeen children, would benefit most from learning. So to her surprise, they informed her one Friday that on the following Monday she could begin making the ten-mile round trip to school, on foot.

A second surprise, as rewarding as it was unexpected, came when Mary discovered that it was not hard to pass along what she learned to her older brothers and sisters. Without realizing it, she was starting her mission in life: to teach other blacks who otherwise would not have an opportunity to learn!

After six years at Scotia Seminary in Concord, North Carolina, with expenses paid by a teacher whom she had never seen, she went to Moody Bible Institute in Chicago for two years. While teaching in missionary schools, usually for short periods, she began dreaming of opening a school of her own, but she never imagined it would be in Florida. By 1923, merger with a school for males produced Bethune-Cookman College.

When the college that had started in a tiny frame house had grown to have an enrollment of about one thousand students, President Franklin D. Roosevelt called upon its founder to help him. As a special advisor to the president on minority affairs, Mrs. Bethune directed the Negro Affairs division of the National Youth Administration. In that and other roles, she was credited with having lifted at least three hundred thousand black Americans out of illiteracy.

As founder and early president of the eight hundred thousand-member National Association of Colored Women, she was hailed as the nation's greatest black woman educator. Eleven universities and colleges conferred honorary degrees upon her, and she retained close ties with Bethune-Cookman College until her death in 1955.

During her lifetime and since, her adopted state has gained reflected glory through her many accomplishments. Nearly every list of "most illustrious American women" includes the name of Mary McLeod Bethune, a daughter of slaves who launched a college with boundless faith and only $1.50 in cash.

25

Speed Capital of the World

Headlines across much of the nation on March 16, 1907, proclaimed racing driver Barney Oldfield "Speed King of the World." Stories from Daytona Beach gave the details. Behind the wheel of his Benz, Oldfield toppled the 128-miles-per-hour record set on the same beach a year earlier by Frank Marriott in his Stanley Steamer.

Even Oldfield could hardly believe the official report. "Sure, I let the great machine have its head," he told reporters. "Though I had earlier had the sensation of seeming to lose my ability to see, it hit me very quickly this time."

He paused, reflected, and added, "Maybe we have about reached the limit of human ability; at 131.7 miles per hour I was practically blind. A dark haze covered everything—even the white sand. I knew that I was about to pass out, so I shut her down—but by then, I was sure that I had traveled faster than any other human on the face of the earth."

The elation of the American driver was heightened by receipt of an overseas telegram reading: "I congratulate a daring Yankee on so remarkable a performance in a German car. Wilhelm."

Never before in racing history had a driver received personal congratulations from any head of state, much less the powerful kaiser of Germany.

Officials of the American Automobile Association were ecstatic. Formed five years earlier by the amalgamation of local and state auto enthusiasts, the national organization

Barney Oldfield behind the wheel of Winton Bullet No. 2, 1904.

took the lead in sponsoring races that had official sanc-
tion. A. R. Pardington, chairman of the AAA, personally
surveyed a number of sites before picking what he said
would become the speed capital of the world.

Some French drivers were risking their necks on a tree-
lined stretch of road between Paris and Orleans. British
record-setters liked the Pendine sands in Wales. Rumor
had it that a dried-up lake north of Cape Town in Africa
offered ideal conditions. Henry Ford, who sponsored
races to boost sales of cars, had tried the ice on Lake St.
Clair near Detroit. There, one of his cars set an AAA
record of 91.4 miles per hour early in 1904.

However, Pardington told newsmen, "Daytona Beach is
superior to any other site presently known. There the
sand is as smooth as glass. It stretches to Ormond, fifteen
miles away, and is so wide that even a blowout seems to
offer little danger."

First held in 1904, the Daytona Beach auto meet became an annual event in which drivers raced against the
clock. In the first Daytona test William K. Vanderbilt
drove a 90-horsepower Mercedes. He easily beat the
American-made Winton Bullet, but he was himself
topped by Oldfield in his 120-horsepower Benz. Vander-

bilt considered himself a winner, anyway, for he broke the
Ford record set on ice fifteen days earlier.

Oldfield knew that in order to better Marriott's 1906
record, he would need another machine. A French
recordsetter, Victor Hemery, had made experimental use
of a huge new 200-horsepower Blitzen Benz. Trading in
his smaller vehicle and adding six thousand dollars in
cash, the man who had started as a cyclist shipped his
purchase directly to Daytona Beach. There he became
"speed king of the world."

After setting the record that brought him a telegram
from Kaiser Wilhelm, Oldfield toured the bars of Ormond.
"You're right," he told one admirer. "I didn't have it on the
floorboard today. That machine would make 150, I'm
sure—but I'm afraid it would be suicide to take it to that
speed. There's a limit to what the human body can take,
you know."

"Wild Bob" Burman shared Oldfield's fear of losing his
sight at extreme speeds. Yet he reached 141 miles per
hour over the measured mile at Daytona Beach in 1911.

Sir Malcolm Campbell's "Bluebird" in a London parade, 1929.

From that time forward, during the next quarter century, the site selected by the American Automobile Association was literally the world capital of speed.

Nearly every spring, enthusiasts who flocked to Daytona were rewarded by a new record of some sort.

Having reached and passed 150 miles per hour at Southport, England, Major Henry Segrave set his eyes on a new goal: 200 miles per hour. Most experts agreed it could not be done; wind resistance could not be overcome past 180 or so.

Segrave did not accept that verdict, so he ordered a new machine for which he wanted an engine of 1,000-horsepower. A French engineer said that so huge an engine would pose problems, but it could be built. However, tires were another matter, he pointed out.

At the Dunlop Company, engineers agreed to try to help Segrave. When they delivered their finished tires to him, they refused to guarantee more than three and one-half minutes' life at 200 miles per hour.

Long before he was ready to make his try for 200 miles per hour, Segrave had told backers that there was only one place in the world where he could hope to set such a record: on the twenty-three-mile Daytona Beach.

Fully testing his immense red Sunbeam for the first time, Segrave was hit by a sudden gust of wind. It threw him into a skid of four hundred yards that ended in the Atlantic Ocean. After putting on a new set of tires, he climbed back into his cockpit and reached 203.70 miles per hour.

Meanwhile, Captain Malcolm Campbell, a distinguished member of Britain's Royal Flying Corps during World War I, had become a major contender. Having been entranced by Maurice Maeterlinck's play *The Bluebird*, he borrowed its title and used it for a succession of ever-faster automobiles.

Segrave's Golden Arrow reached 231.45 miles per hour at Daytona Beach in 1929, but two years later—on the same beach—Campbell's Bluebird was clocked at 246.09 miles per hour. Both drivers were knighted in recognition

Daytona is one of the few great beaches where automobiles are still permitted, for a small fee.

of their achievements, but neither was satisfied.

Sir Malcolm broke the 250 miles per hour barrier, long regarded as the ultimate, at Daytona Beach in 1932. His new record had hardly been flashed around the world before he set his eyes upon a new one, 300 miles per hour. He tried for it annually, but after boosting his old mark by only four miles per hour in 1935, he decided that the ultimate speed had been reached on the beach. Wheelspin developed in the range of 250 miles per hour, and winds and waves sometimes created tiny ridges in the sand.

This dilemma sent Campbell and others to the salt flats of Utah and to Africa's Verneuk Pan. Having reigned supreme in the world of speed for almost thirty years, Daytona Beach was abruptly abandoned by those seeking new records.

But the heritage lives today. When you visit the beach where two racing drivers set the records that brought knighthood to them, you will find that automobiles sometimes seem to outnumber humans on the sand.

26

The Dixie Bee Propelled the Nation into the Highway Age

"Frankly, I see our great Dixie highway as only the start. Once it is in use, a year from now, other regions will envy us and get busy, too. Sooner than any of us think, we will have a great pattern of highways that will make automobile travel possible throughout our entire nation."

Clark Howell, chairman of the Dixie Highway Association during a three-day meeting in Chattanooga, Tennessee, was jubilant. "We have settled upon a great loop," he said, "that will give travelers the choice between a western and an eastern route. Within months, we will begin to see a great flow of vehicles from Chicago to Miami, and from Miami to Chicago, as well."

The editor of the Atlanta *Constitution* and a long-time member of the Democratic National Committee, Howell had enough influential and wealthy friends to be confident of success. Under his guidance, commissioners from seven states selected key cities to be served by the proposed highway.

Their timetable for its completion—one year—seems naive from the perspective of seventy-five years. But in 1915 people advocating the construction of a highway did not think in terms of concrete freeways with exit ramps and immense bridges. They envisioned the use of mule-drawn earth-moving equipment that would dig and scrape a narrow trail for gasoline-powered vehicles to traverse.

"Carl Fisher is the father of the movement," the Atlanta editor said whenever he rose to speak about the visionary

In many places where cars became hopelessly trapped, farm folk gathered to watch mules pull them from the mud.

project. "His major business interests are in Indianapolis, Indiana. There he is president of the Indianapolis Motor Speedway and the Prest-O-Lite Company.

"Mr. Fisher first visited Florida, I believe, in his capacity as chairman of the touring board of the American Automobile Association. He was so impressed with the future potential of Miami that he began purchasing land. He expects soon to begin building a great hotel there, and already has other business interests in the city."

Like most visitors of that time, Fisher usually reached the city of Julia Tuttle and Henry Flagler by rail. But his passionate interest in automobiles, linked with his role as president of the Fisher Automobile Company in Indianapolis, caused him to see Florida's level terrain as "just right for the terminus of a great highway."

As a member of the Trail Blazers, Fisher went on the first transcontinental automobile tour. He watched with great interest the rapid rise of special tours sponsored by the Glidden Company, and in 1910 he cheered enthusiastically when he heard that a contingent of automobiles had succeeded in reaching New York from Atlanta in less than one week.

If Henry M. Flagler's railroad could transform the east coast of Florida, a great system of highways stretching all the way to Chicago would double, maybe even treble, the number of persons who would come to his proposed hotel, he reasoned. Thus Carl Fisher organized what he called "a safari." Associates, business friends, and a few daring auto enthusiasts responded to his 1914 call to form the Dixie Highway Pathfinders. From the start, they planned not only to motor from Chicago to Miami but to develop plans for a highway linking the two cities.

The vehicles driven by Fisher and his Pathfinders and other early adventurers represented many makes: Pope-Hartford, Pacemaker, Columbia, Cadillac, Locomobile, even a Matheson complete with a glass hood touted as making it all but impossible to hear the "silent six" motor in action.

The Dixie Pathfinders had easy going through Gary, Indiana, and south to Indianapolis. Distances began to test tires and motors as they reached and passed Louisville. South of that city, their real troubles began.

At least one woman made the historic Atlanta to New York tour in 1910.

Advance teams had gone ahead, erecting poles where there were no trees suitable for marking with strips of white cloth. Members of these teams told reporters that they had made the route so clear that "no driver can fail to find the way." Yet one driver wandered so far off course that he never rejoined the safari, and another was lost for more than a day.

Their troubles were minor by comparison with those caused by heavy rains. Some makeshift roads were flooded so deeply that cars stalled. When the water receded, deep mud caused wheels to spin helplessly until teams of mules were brought to pull cars and drivers to solid ground.

In spite of floods, breakdowns, and blowouts, Carl Fisher and his fellow trailblazers triumphantly roared down the streets of Miami about ten days after leaving Chicago. Their safari led to the Chattanooga convention at which the Dixie Highway Association was formally organized.

In Chattanooga, Carl Fisher received wild applause when he affirmed, "We did not pilot our automobiles all that distance as an advertising scheme. We certainly did not make the trip as a joy ride. We want to see a great highway linking the Atlantic Coast with the Great Lakes—for the benefit of every state here represented!"

Readers of the Jacksonville *Sunday Times-Union* were ecstatic on May 23, 1915, when they learned that Jacksonville would be a key city in "the Dixie Highway from the Great Lakes to the Gulf of Mexico." Exuberance reigned in Tallahassee, too; but in central Florida gloom quickly turned into anger. Promoters and business leaders then reasoned, correctly, that if the new highway bypassed their region, they would reap no economic benefits from it. Therefore, they organized "probably the greatest road convention ever held in Florida." Assembled at Kissimmee on May 8, more than two thousand delegates decided that they would work to "turn the routing of the Dixie Highway through Central Florida."

They got nowhere with their effort. The plans already adopted in Chattanooga held firm, but the timetable of

A child offered flowers to the driver of a mighty Columbia.

those who framed them proved optimistic. It took years, not months, to create an unbroken highway linking Chicago with Miami. By the time it was completed, it had become generally known as the "Dixie Bee," and its western loop projected to include Michigan had been abandoned as unfeasible.

Snaking around lakes and swamps in Florida and hills in Georgia and Tennessee, twisting miles off course to cross major streams where bridges already existed, the Dixie Bee never actually permitted "driving from Miami to Chicago along a bee line."

Crude as it was by standards set later in the century, the highway did more than bring an economic boom to Miami and to many other Florida cities along the route. It showed the feasibility of linking half a dozen states to benefit each through gasoline-powered travel. In this sense the crooked little Dixie Bee was the progenitor of today's gigantic interstate highway system.

Eventually given a hard surface for its entire length, the brain child of Miami Beach developer Carl Fisher saw additional segments incorporated into the fledgling federal highway system. Today those stretches of the original highway still in use are seldom identified as having been part of it. But the auto traveler who ventures off the interstate in Florida, Georgia, or Tennessee—and even rural Indiana—will occasionally find a visual reminder in a restaurant still boldly labeled: "Dixie Bee Cafe."

27

A Gift to the Nation from an Immigrant

The inspiration for the Sanctuary and the Tower came of that stuff of which dreams are made. The Two combined a dream to carry on the work of my grandfather, who a hundred years ago transformed a grim desert island in the North Sea into a bower of green verdure to which the birds came which made the island famous.

But an inspiration is of little value if it is not carried into realization. I was fortunate to enlist Frederick Law Olmsted for the Sanctuary and Milton B. Medary for the Tower. I wanted to present to the American people what has been so often called "The Taj Mahal of America"—a spot which would reach out in its beauty through the superbly beautiful architecture of the Tower, through the music of the bells, to the people and fill their souls with the quiet, the repose, the influence of the beautiful.

—Edward Bok

That description of what is now famous as Bok Tower Gardens, written not long before the donor's death, offers a rare glimpse at the inner life of a very private man.

Born in the Netherlands in 1863, Edward Bok came to New York with his father and mother aboard the ocean liner *The Queen*.

There was nothing regal about their life in Brooklyn, however, for no job awaited the father, and the health of the mother declined rapidly. Edward and his brother spent many evenings with baskets, searching the streets for pieces of wood and bits of coal to keep a fire going in their decaying home.

Like Thomas Edison, Bok found a job as an office boy

for the Western Union Telegraph Company. To him it seemed a great improvement over window cleaning at fifty cents a week. As a self-taught stenographer, he worked for publishing firms before becoming editor of the *Brooklyn Magazine.* From that post, he founded his own press syndicate, then became editor of *The Ladies Home Journal.*

While turning out a series of popular books, Edward Bok pushed the magazine he edited to top circulation in the world: more than one million copies. At his retirement in 1919, he found himself wealthy and restless.

A visit to Lake Wales convinced him that he had found what would become an American mecca. He bought a parcel of land in 1922, knowing exactly what he wished to do with it.

Earlier, he had returned to Europe and had been amazed to find that his grandfather and grandmother had left a lasting imprint on an island about five miles off the Dutch coast. Sent there by King William as a mayor-judge, the elder Bok and his wife had been told to rid the island of pirates and "wreckers." Shipwrecks, plundered by wreckers, made the island a place hated by seamen of the region.

Bok the elder not only got rid of pirates and wreckers, he also planted trees, cleared out debris, and made a sanctuary for sea birds and migrating land birds.

Editor, author, philanthropist Edward W. Bok [DICTIONARY OF AMERICAN PORTRAITS]

His grandson, an intimate friend of Theodore Roosevelt
and already beginning to accumulate a great fortune, had
what he called a vision when he first visited the island
transformed by his grandfather. When he found Lake
Wales he finally knew how to respond to that vision.

Once Bok had acquired more than 130 acres in a tract
that included the highest point on the peninsula of Flor-
dia, he employed the finest landscape gardener and architect he could find. Frederick Law Olmsted, noted in his
own right, was the son of the man who designed Central
Park in New York, the grounds of the Biltmore Estate near
Asheville, North Carolina, and Druid Hills in Atlanta,
Georgia. Architect Milton B. Medary was internationally
known for innovative designs.

Although he never gave reporters information about
how much he expected to spend, it was soon clear that
Bok had no limits in mind. By the time his two chief aides
had completed their work in 1929, the Bok Singing Tower
and surrounding gardens were unlike anything else in the
world.

Atop a 295-foot hillock—the highest point in the
state—Medary placed a 205-foot tower of Georgia granite
and tan coquina such as that used to build St. Augustine's
old fort. Stone pelicans, geese, flamingos, and swans
adorn the tower, which is crowned with herons shown
rearing their young.

Inside the tower there are fifty-three finely tuned
bronze bells cast in England. The smallest weighs 17
pounds, while the largest is 318 times as heavy (more
than 5,500 pounds). Instead of swinging, and being lim-
ited to a narrow range of sounds, each bell is played from
a keyboard. As a result, a carillonneur can achieve subtle
shadings as well as great dramatic power.

Calvin Coolidge came to Lake Wales on February 1,
1929, as a representative of all Americans. There he dedi-
cated the tower and gardens created by a Dutch immigrant
"as a gift for visitation by the American people in gratitude for the opportunity they had given him."

Edward Bok survived the dedication of his gift less than

a year. His grave on the lawn of his winter home is marked by a stone bearing only his name and the dates of his birth and death. At the immense tower he built within sight of the grave, the biggest of the bronze bells—called the Bourdon—is inscribed: "This Carillon is a tribute of affection from Edward William Bok to his grandparents: Lovers of Beauty. Nineteen Hundred and Twenty-Six."

Trustees of the foundation established by Bok have enlarged the surrounding gardens, but they adamantly refuse to disturb the natural beauty of the Florida landscape. When a tree dies, it is not cut. When it falls, it is permitted to lie where it is "until it returns to the soil that nourished it."

Noted naturalist John Burroughs, who came back again and again once he had discovered this sanctuary, summed up his visits in sixteen words: "I come here to find myself. It is so easy to get lost in the world."

Several days a week during most months, a noted carillonneur gives a concert at 3:00 P.M. Taped music can be heard at any time, and the gardens are open every day of the year. Located fifty-five miles south of Orlando and three miles north of Lake Wales, the sanctuary for auditory and visual beauty is near the crossroads of U.S. highway 27 and state highway 60. For additional information write to P. O. Box 3810, Lake Wales, FL; telephone (813) 676-1154 or (813) 676-1408.

28

Key West Was Home to Hemingway

Back in the "good old days" before television, the big entertainment in the sleepy little town of Key West was the weekly prize fight held in the old arena once used for cockfights when the town had been a cigar-making center. Spectators sat on bare pine board bleachers and only bet among themselves.

Suddenly, in 1929, it began to be suspected that dirty dealings had started, that some fighters (they were all nonprofessionals) were throwing fights, for a price.

One Saturday night the big favorite suddenly fell to his knees. A spectator, a self-appointed vigilante, jumped into the ring, grabbed the fighter who had struck a foul blow unseen by most of the audience, and grimly spoke to him. Immediately the boy raced to the center of the ring and shouted the confession, "I did it! I fouled him!"

A wave of huzzahs erupted from the stands in honor of the alert citizen who had settled the problem. His name was Ernest Hemingway.

The writer's "Key West period" began in 1928 when he and his pregnant second wife, Pauline, returned from Europe wanting to find a relaxing, inexpensive place to live, work, and raise children—and to fish. An old book he had read on fishing in Florida had suggested Key West to Hemingway.

In their yellow Model-A Ford convertible coupe, the Hemingways drove and ferried to the southernmost town in the United States, a sleepy, almost-forgotten little spot peopled mainly by small-time commercial fishermen and their families. The last big excitement there had been the

Tennessee Williams in
Key West, about 1960
[UNIVERSITY OF TEXAS
AT AUSTIN]

Spanish-American War thirty years earlier when Key West was the place for coaling steamers and dispatching news.

A century earlier when the artist John James Audubon had arrived looking for pink flamingos, the now-quiet village had been a booming seaport.

After living in several rental places, in 1931 the Hemingways bought an old Spanish house built in 1851 opposite the lighthouse. They modernized it, adding a pool house with showers and dressing rooms and an upstairs workroom for Hemingway. The author contributed personal touches that revealed his lifelong preoccupation with struggle: a Spanish birthing chair, a silent reminder of the pain with which life begins; a statue of a bullfighter, symbolizing the ever-present life-or-death drama of living; a mounted head of a wildebeest shot on his first African safari, showing that even the fleetest of foot cannot always escape the hunter; and a model of the Civil War ironclad *Monitor*, proclaiming, "Here is the home of a man fascinated by war."

Then there were the cats, six-toed ones, that soon became multigenerational. More than forty of their descendants still live at the same address, 907 Whitehead Street.

Son Patrick was born to the Hemingways in 1928 and Gregory in 1931.

Meanwhile *A Farewell to Arms* was finished, first handwritten because Hemingway refused to use a typewriter, then copied by a secretary.

While Key West was a good place to work, it was also a very good place to enjoy life. For the Hemingways that meant fishing. One of Ernest's fishing cronies was Josey Russell, owner of the bar off Duval Street and a regular rum runner between Cuba and the Keys. He introduced the author to marlin fishing in the Gulf Stream out of Havana, possibly one source of inspiration for *The Old Man and the Sea* that was published years later. It is known that Josey was translated into the character of Harry Morgan in *To Have and Have Not*, which was written and set in Key West.

As Leicester Hemingway recalled in *My Brother, Ernest Hemingway*, the fishing parties would be well-stocked with gin, key limes, sugar, and ice water. "Papa" Hemingway's preferred costume always was a blue-striped Basque fishing shirt and beltless khaki pants. "One horrified local lady declared," Leicester remembered, "that he always looked like he'd just pulled his pants on and planned to pull them off again any second."

The Hemingways did not remain in Florida constantly. They traveled out West, to Cuba, to Europe and Africa. When the Spanish Civil War broke out in 1936, he went to Spain.

The next summer, 1937, as he was preparing to return to cover the war for the North American Newspaper Alliance, a visitor came to Key West. Leicester Hemingway recorded that magazine writer Martha Gellhorn walked into Sloppy Joe's bar, saw Ernest's name on one of the bar stools, and asked when the author might be expected. "It's almost three o'clock. If he's in town, he'll be coming in," the bartender replied.

Ms. Gellhorn, a statuesque blonde, waited and got her interview. She also got her man, as she became the third Mrs. Ernest Hemingway in 1940. Hemingway did not re-

Hemingway's upright Royal typewriter [HEMINGWAY HOUSE AND MUSEUM]

turn to live in Florida. Pauline, the second Mrs. Hemingway, received the Key West house in the divorce settlement.

Other writers had ties to Key West. In 1926 the poet Hart Crane, while staying on Cuba's Isle of Pines, wrote many of his poems later collected as *Key West: An Island Sheaf* and published posthumously.

In the early 1940s, playwright Tennessee Williams drifted around the country working at odd jobs and picking up impressions of people and places that became the raw materials of his plays, such as *The Glass Menagerie, A Streetcar Named Desire, Cat on a Hot Tin Roof, Camino Real,* and *The Rose Tattoo.* For a while he lived in Key West where he said he had a "love affair with a fishing village barely out of sight of Havana."

Today, the fast-growing city is such a tourist mecca that the Chamber of Commerce often does not bother to reply to letters of inquiry. The Ernest Hemingway home and museum, open daily, affords an intimate insight into the life of "Papa" Hemingway. For more information in preparation for a visit that demands at least two hours, address inquiries to 907 Whitehead Street, Key West, FL; telephone (305) 294-1576.

29

FDR Was Saved by the Wife of a Miami Physician

"Mr. Roosevelt talked only about two minutes—extending his greetings to the people of the Florida East Coast.

"Then he got back into his open automobile, about fifteen feet away. He had hardly settled in the back seat when I got up from the bench where I was sitting, in order to get a better look.

"That's when this fellow—dark, with curly hair—stood up on the same bench. Since the bench was made to fold in the middle, I thought I might fall. So I turned around and said, 'Please stand still; you're about to knock me off the bench!'

"That's when I first saw he had a pistol in his hand. I think I must have cried out, 'O my God, he's going to kill Mr. Roosevelt!' At the same time, I switched my handbag to my left arm and used my right hand to grab him and twist his arm upward."

Pausing in her story to respond to a question from a Miami reporter, Mrs. Lillian Cross pondered and then slowly shook her head. "I'm sorry," she said, "I really don't know how many shots were fired or who they hit. But I do know that his gun was pointed right at Mr. Roosevelt, over my shoulder. After I grabbed him, I don't know exactly what did happen."

When met by physician-surgeon Dr. W. F. Cross, his hundred-pound wife was visibly shaken, but smiling. Almost instantly, he noticed that her right cheek was grimy, marked by gunpowder from the pistol of the man who

Voter dissatisfaction with economic ills contributed largely to F.D.R.'s smashing victory in 1932.

nearly succeeded in killing the president-elect, Franklin D. Roosevelt, on February 15, 1933.

Sent to the White House by popular mandate in the election of 1932, Roosevelt planned to relax during the weeks before his March inauguration. With the Great Depression gripping the nation, he would have little time for relaxation once he took the oath of office.

Thus he accepted the invitation of wealthy Vincent Astor for an extended fishing trip in southern waters. Eleven days after having boarded the yacht *Nourmahal*, Roosevelt docked at Pier 1 in Miami Harbor. Plans called for him to make a brief personal appearance in Bayfront Park, accompanied by political allies headed by Chicago's Mayor Anton Cermak.

Riding in an open car, the president-elect was delighted to see an estimated fifteen thousand people waiting for him, with the Dade County Courthouse in the background. Sixty Miami policemen were stationed in the park, and one hundred more were posted along streets through which a motorcycle escort of twenty uniformed men led the motorcade. Six Secret Service operatives headed by Capt. J. H. Reidy made Roosevelt's personal bodyguard feel "pushed aside." Yet Reidy remained as close to the president-elect as circumstances permitted.

Soon after Roosevelt's election to the nation's highest office, Vice President-elect John Garner, had warned him that he could expect attempts upon his life. Smiling, FDR repeated a Theodore Roosevelt quotation that Garner had heard before: "The only real danger from an assassin is from one who does not care whether he loses his own life in the act or not. Most of the crazy ones can be spotted first."

Because that mood of confidence extended to aides who traveled with Roosevelt, when shots were fired in the bright Florida sunshine, one of them thought he had heard a car backfire. Roosevelt later admitted that he heard the sound, but attributed it to a firecracker. By the time the sound was repeated four more times, almost everyone in Bayfront Park knew that a pistol was being fired.

Chicago's Mayor Cermak, said spectators, was knocked from the running board of the open automobile by the first shot. He dropped to the ground, where he twisted in agony while the gunman emptied his weapon.

In addition to mortally wounded Cermak, four other people were hit by one or more of the five bullets that were fired. William Sinnott, once a New York City policeman, was shot in the head. So was twenty-two-year-old Russell Caldwell of Miami. Mrs. Joe H. Gill, wife of the president of the Florida Power and Light Company, was shot through the abdomen and was listed as in critical condition. Margaret Kruis, visiting from New Jersey, escaped with a minor injury to her hand.

Aware only that she had saved the life of the president-elect, Lillian Cross was bowled over by spectators who rushed to seize the gunman. "Kill him! Kill him!" they yelled as they converged upon Giuseppe Zangara, the would-be assassin.

From his seat in the automobile, Roosevelt shouted at the top of his lungs that he was not hurt. "Leave the poor fellow to the police," he ordered. The men who had seized Zangara obeyed, wordless.

Ready to talk—even eager—the gunman was sufficiently lucid to say he was glad he had hit Cermak. He hated all persons of power and wealth, he told Miami detectives. In Italy, which he had left only a few years earlier, he had seen the rich and powerful send their children to school, while children of poor men like his father went to work mending shoes and baking bread.

Drifting about Miami, the unemployed bricklayer chanced upon a pawn shop where he bought a .32 caliber pistol for eight dollars. A newspaper story about the upcoming visit of the president-elect to Miami had prompted him to spend his last cash to purchase the weapon.

"I tried to get to the park early," he told police. "I thought that it would be easy to get close to him, but lots of people were there ahead of me.

President Franklin Delano Roosevelt

"I sat on a bench, waiting, and my stomach—where I had a big operation that left this scar—kept aching worse than ever. I planned to hit Roosevelt while he was talking, but he sat down very soon and I couldn't get a good shot through the people in front of me."

Zangara, who was only five feet, one inch tall, waited until spectators in front of him tired and sat down. "That gave me my big chance," he said. "I stood up on my bench and took good aim at Mr. Roosevelt. When the bench started to wobble, a little lady grabbed me. I think she must have tried to choke me. Anyway, I got off five shots, but I knew that I had missed my man."

On the twenty-first floor of the Dade County Courthouse where the jail was located, Zangara was questioned by psychiatrists. They agreed that he was very strange, but they were not sure he could not be tried.

Meanwhile, Mrs. Eleanor Roosevelt received the news in New York City from a butler who stammered with excitement. Learning that her husband was not injured, she told reporters, "These things are to be expected." Later she placed a telephone call and managed to reach her husband at the bedside of Anton Cermak.

They talked briefly, then Mrs. Roosevelt told reporters and friends, "He's all right; he isn't even excited." Shortly afterward, accompanied only by her maid, the first lady-to-be boarded a train bound for Ithaca, New York, to fill a speaking engagement.

Security was beefed up immediately. In Miami, Roosevelt's guard detail was doubled. In Washington, Richard Jarvis sent Secret Service agents to augment the two-man force then guarding the White House "in spite of the fact that President Hoover had retired for the night." In New York, where Roosevelt soon reported to keep a speaking engagement at the Hotel Astor, 550 police were detailed to prevent another assassination attempt.

Without exception, professional lawmen who studied the bizarre events in Miami agreed that had it not been for diminutive Lillian Cross, the nation might never have had what came to be called the New Deal. Robert P. Gore of

Philadelphia, a longtime friend of the president-elect, was standing by the automobile when Zangara began shooting. He told reporters for the Philadelphia Record, "It happened so suddenly that practically everyone was stunned into inaction." But, he added, while bewildered professionals tried to see what was taking place, "a woman threw her arms around the assailant's neck and tried to strangle him while he was still shooting."

That vivid description may have been somewhat embellished, but there was never any doubt about the significance of the actions of the Florida housewife. From New York, Roosevelt sent Lillian Cross a two hundred-word telegram of thanks for her "prompt and courageous action." Congressman Green of Florida proposed in the House of Representatives that she be awarded the Congressional Medal of Honor for heroism in a moment of crisis.

When Anton Cermak died, the charge against Zangara was changed to murder, followed by a swift trial. He was executed on March 20, barely five weeks after the attempted assassination.

Four months after Zangara went to the electric chair, headlines of the nation were dominated by FDR's proposals to aid millions of Americans made penniless by the Great Depression. Concurrently, Representative Allgood of Alabama was pleased when his colleagues approved a resolution he had introduced. It solemnly expressed "thanks and grateful appreciation to Mrs. W. F. Cross of Miami" for her role in making it possible for a stricken America to benefit from the New Deal.

30

Zora Hurston's Black Folklore Was Far Ahead of Its Time

Maybe a few tourists in their Model-A Fords had an idea that Eatonville was special, but they would have been hard pressed to say why. Many residents and a few outsiders could have told them that it was America's first truly black community, complete with a charter, mayor, city council, and town marshal.

In the mid 1930s, almost anyone in Eatonville would have said that one of the young women of the town was different in a way that hardly anyone understood. When she wanted to do so, she could talk like the college graduate she was; but most of the time she spoke just like her neighbors who had quit school in the fifth grade.

She did not seem to know what it meant to hold an honest job, and lots of the time you could find her loafing around the general store listening to menfolk who sat around trying to outdo each other in telling whoppers.

The editors at J. B. Lippincott & Company did not quite know what to make of Zora Hurston, either. They knew she could make a sentence sing, and they realized that she was working a vein of literary ore that no earlier prospector had discovered, but the black folklore she sent to them did not seem to have much appeal for a book market that was almost 100 percent white.

Zora Hurston was at least thirty years ahead of her time. While she described her Florida home town as "burly, boiling, hard-hitting, rugged-individualistic," she may not have seen that her adjectives applied to herself, too. With a B.A. degree from Barnard College, she could have written to please white folks. Instead, she chose to incorporate tall tales and hoodoo (*not* voodoo—that is what whites say) rituals, every-day sayings, and songs into novels, short stories, essays, articles, and her autobiography.

Never really sure when she was born, Zora thought perhaps her birthday was January 7,1903. Although that date probably was wrong, she was right in saying that when her mother delivered without the aid of a midwife, the baby girl "just rushed out by herself."

Most of her life, Zora stayed in a rush.

When she heard that a member of a Gilbert and Sullivan troupe wanted to hire a maid, she rushed over and got the job—before learning that it would require her to leave Florida. Once she was in the distant North, she found that Howard University in Washington, D.C., would let her attend, part-time.

At Howard in 1923, she saw her first literary effort published in *Stylus* magazine. Along with later pieces, it helped her gain a scholarship to Barnard College. By the time she graduated, her original style and source material brought her to the attention of the internationally noted anthropologist Franz Boas.

Back in her native South, she rushed to collect and publish folklore, pausing in her pursuit only long enough to teach drama for a season at Mary McLeod Bethune's college in Daytona Beach.

Three books in four years brought her two Guggenheim fellowships to collect folklore in Jamaica, Bermuda, and Haiti. By that time, she was working on her autobiography and making plans to go to work for Franklin D. Roosevelt's WPA, again collecting black folklore.

Many of her brief stories, largely passed orally from generation to generation until she put them into print, involve a hero who is invariably named John. According to her, "John (not John Henry) is the great culture hero in Negro folk-lore."

In an era when few black Americans called themselves "black," Zora wrote that John "is like Daniel in Jewish folk-lore, the wish-fulfillment hero of the race. The one

Zora Neale Hurston admitted in private that her smile "sometimes looked as if it was pasted on." [COURTESY OF EVERETTE HURSTON]

who, nevertheless, or in spite of laughter, usually defeats Ole Massa, God, and the Devil."

Blacks, she said, habitually—almost unconsciously— use laughter as a disguise. "The brother in black puts a laugh in every vacant place in his mind. His laugh has a hundred meanings. It may mean amusement, anger, grief, bewilderment, chagrin, curiosity, simple pleasure, or any other of the known or undefined emotions."

Small wonder, therefore, that her stories, which have much more impact when spoken aloud than when read silently, are packed with laughter. She tells of a man "so ugly till they had to spread a sheet over his head so sleep could slip up on him." Many of her collected stories begin and end with brief poetry having much in common with nonsense rhymes published for whites as "children's books":

> Well, once upon a time
> was good ole time;
> Monkey chew tobacco
> and spit white lime.

Describing her plan to visit New Orleans to collect hoodoo lore, she reported, "I headed my toe-nails toward Louisiana."

Although taken more seriously outside Florida than within her native state, she was never widely known during her life. Not until her death in 1960 did anyone discover that she had published more books than any other black woman in America.

Beginning in the 1970s, a revival of interest in the woman and her work has coincided with radical changes in attitudes of whites toward blacks, and of blacks toward themselves. When the entire body of her literary output is surveyed, it is clear that in her books she tried to do for her people what the *Foxfire* series has done for whites of Appalachia.

When Zora Hurston collected, wrote, polished, and published, she was a black woman in a white man's world. Instead of winning a small fraction of the enormous financial success of *Foxfire,* the Eatonville native found brief jobs as a maid, a librarian, and as a reporter for the Fort Pierce *Chronicle.*

Although the date of her birth is uncertain, there is no doubt that she died on January 28, 1960. That official record comes from her final residence, the County Welfare Home at Fort Pierce.

31

Ding Darling Saved Sanibel After He Was Buried

Long-time friends had no difficulty in recognizing Ding Darling in spite of the fact that the figure depicted in a cartoon had an ethereal quality. Walking through a door that opened from an office cluttered with stacks of paper, Darling waved his hat. " 'Bye now—it's been wonderful knowing you," read the caption.

Michigan native Jay Norwood Darling, dead at age eighty-five, had long ago made arrangements with his secretary. A cartoon from his pen, entrusted to her, was reproduced soon after his funeral. Then it was mailed to a long list of friends on Captiva Island, Sanibel Island, and elsewhere.

The two-time Pulitzer Prize-winning cartoonist, universally known as Ding, spent his last years in disappointment. A few who knew him well said he came perilously close to being bitter. After years of struggling to save swamps, mangrove forests, and pristine beaches from developers, he gave up the fight. Convinced that he would never win, he sold every acre he owned on the Florida island that he had long called home.

At the time he sold, it appeared that he was right. In spite of years of effort, he had failed to persuade the Florida legislature to protect precious wetlands and the wildlife they sheltered. But the nationally renowned cartoonist did not reckon on the influence of his friends. Joined by many others who knew a little about him, those who received his "goodbye cartoon" set out to accomplish in his memory what he had failed to do in life.

160

Born less than twelve months after Florida's vote gave the White House to Rutherford B. Hayes in 1876, Darling worked briefly as a reporter. Then his natural talent with the pen surfaced and elevated him to the role of political cartoonist. In Des Moines, Iowa, he became staff cartoonist for the *Register* in 1906 and held the post for forty-three years, being nationally syndicated by the New York *Herald Tribune.* It was as a wanderer from far away Iowa that he first saw Captiva Island in 1936. With his wife, Penny, he soaked up local legends that said the island was used by the pirate Blackbeard as a place to imprison his captives. The adjoining island, Sanibel, he soon learned, got its name from another pirate. José Gaspar, who used those waters as his home base during part of the eighteenth century, was an ardent subject of Spain's queen, popularly called Santa Isabella. In her honor he named the lush semitropical island Sanibel.

Today, Sanibel is world famous as "the shell capital of North America." Visitors spend so much time combing beaches that many of them soon develop what natives call the "Sanibel Stoop." No other place on the continent offers such diversity and profusion of sea shells.

Nearby Captiva, where Ding Darling and his wife built their winter home, is famous—or infamous—as "the mosquito capital of the world." Insects breed in salt marshes so prolifically that early evening clouds of them look to first-time visitors much like predawn fog in the Smoky Mountains.

Long before he became a Floridian by adoption, Darling had made a reputation as a conservationist who worked with the Izaak Walton League, the National Audubon Society, and the National Wildlife Foundation. On Captiva, one of his proudest accomplishments was the successful digging of a well that provided fresh water for birds.

Only a few months after the life of Franklin D. Roosevelt was saved by a one-hundred-pound Miami woman, the president called Ding Darling to Washington. At his insistence, the cartoonist agreed to become head of the U.S. Biological Survey, predecessor agency of the U.S.

Fish and Wildlife Service.

In Washington Darling managed to add four million acres to the federal system of wildlife refuges. Almost casually, he executed for sale to hunters a revenue stamp that depicted a bird familiar to him from childhood: a duck. That launched the famous duck stamps, now the focus of annual competition by artists.

Ding did not fare nearly so well in his beloved Florida as he did in Washington. Much of Captiva Island belonged to state agencies whose executives almost casually sold mangrove and hummock land for development. In vain, he tried for years to persuade members of the legislature to turn part of the island into a national refuge for tropical birds. Their refusal eventually led him to give up in disgust and shake the sand of Florida off his feet.

Ding's body was buried for only a few days before his final cartoon reached friends who were so moved by it that they began to talk of implementing his long-time dream. Prodded by them, Gov. Farris Bryant endorsed a plan to create a memorial to the conservationist on Sanibel Island.

From the start, the Jay N. ("Ding") Darling Memorial Committee wanted more than a token memorial. A tiny plot, designated as a refuge, was gratefully accepted as a gift, but Ding's friends wanted him to be commemorated by a tract "big enough for the man's big, big heart."

Expanding from the original 3.31 acres, the Ding Darling Refuge gradually encompassed islands in Matlacha Pass, Pine Island Sound, the Caloosahatchee River, and even Tampa Bay. State-owned land within the sanctuary was turned over to the federal authorities in 1967, leading to a congressional appropriation for the purchase of privately owned land.

By 1970 the J. N. "Ding" Darling National Wildlife Refuge—largest of its kind anywhere—was spread across nearly five thousand acres. Relatives and friends of Darling who lived in Des Moines added their influence and money to efforts of Floridians.

Today the memorial refuge made up largely of wetlands and island uplands is administered from Sanibel Island. Anything under a full day is hopelessly inadequate to sample the canoe trail, birdwatching tower, marinas, and wildlife drive. Additional nature trails and displays are available at the Sanibel-Captiva Conservation Center not far from the entrance to the refuge. For full information call (813) 472-1100 in order to contact the headquarters of the refuge. Staff members of the conservation center may be reached at (813) 472-2329.

32

Marjorie Kinnan Rawlings Wrote of Florida Crackers

"You're looking at a landed proprietor!"

Guests of aspiring writer Marjorie Kinnan Rawlings reacted with the surprise she had expected. "I'm serious," she continued. "I now own 3,992 orange trees spread over nearly seventy acres."

Rochester, New York, friends waited to hear more.

"My orange grove is near Hawthorne, Florida," their hostess at an informal luncheon explained. "My husband and I call our place Cross Creek. I'm not going to tell you what we paid for it. I'd be ashamed for you to know."

Only three years earlier, in 1925, Florida was at the height of a real estate boom. Especially on the lower east coast, speculators were making fortunes in weeks, sometimes in days. But the hurricane of 1926 was followed by an even more severe one in 1928. Land values plummeted, and per capita income in the state was said to have dropped below three hundred dollars per year. Well before the Wall Street crash of 1929, Florida was prostrate.

Desperation of the natives provided splendid opportunities for newcomers like the bright young woman from Rochester. True to her initial comment, she never revealed how little she paid for her splendid orange grove, which she envisioned as an ideal place in which to write without disturbance.

"I hate cities," she told her neighbors when she moved to Cross Creek. "I was born in Washington, D.C., and as a little girl I hated every minute I had to spend on those hot streets. Down here, I'm really going to live!"

Marjorie Kinnan had earned her first money at age eleven—two dollars from the Washington *Post* for a story entered in a contest—but after graduation from the University of Wisconsin as a Phi Beta Kappa, she worked as a newspaper reporter while amassing a file of rejection slips for her fiction writing.

Nevertheless, her husband, Charles Rawlings, encouraged her to "keep on trying and see if you can't find a fresh environment from which to write."

Exploring the scrub country of north Florida, the city-reared woman discovered a lifestyle seldom noticed by tourists and winter residents. Tiny clusters of impoverished whites, usually second- or third-generation Floridians, eked out a living in hummocks scattered among the swamps.

Just two years after having chosen Florida as her adopted state, Mrs. Rawlings sold to *Scribner's Magazine* a series of vignettes. Their title, "Cracker Chidlings," attracted Scribner's famed book editor, Maxwell Perkins, who also was literary mentor to Ernest Hemingway and William Faulkner. He cautiously encouraged the aspiring novelist who lived about as far from Key West as she could get and still remain in Florida.

This, in turn, caused Mrs. Rawlings to startle her husband with an announcement. "I'm going to have to be

Marjorie Kinnan Rawlings, after having achieved fame as a novelist.

away for a while. I found a family up in the Big Scrub that
will let me stay with them. You'll have to do the best you
can; there's no other way I can learn how these people
dress and eat, talk and think."

Charles Rawlings and his wife, who had experienced
earlier tensions, parted company after having agreed that
their only course of action was a divorce. Before the de-
cree was final, she was established in a moonshiner's
cabin nearly hidden from view by a lush forest of sweet
gums, hickory trees, live oaks, and magnolias.

In that setting the woman who spent her formative
years in the nation's capital found the isolation she
craved, plus the color, cadence, and unremitting despair
of Florida cracker life in the 1930s. (A "cracker" is a poor
white person of the southeastern United States.) Perhaps
without realizing what was happening, she also absorbed
the fatalism that dominated life in the backwoods.

Things happened, she found out, and there was not any
use "to get all lathered up" about them. It would not make
a bit of difference. Once this attitude pervaded her being,
Marjorie Rawlings was ready to write *The Yearling.* Published in 1938, it caused many a Floridian to walk the
streets with new pride. When on earth had a woman
writer of the state had such an honor as winning a Pulitzer
Prize?

When *The Yearling* was purchased by Metro-Goldwyn-
Mayer to become a motion picture, the region of scrub
trees, moonshine stills, and Florida crackers took on fresh
importance nationally, but also in Florida.

Now a celebrity both at home in Florida and throughout
the land, Marjorie Kinnan Rawlings received honorary
degrees from Rollins College, the University of Florida,
and the University of Tampa in 1942. After achieving literary success, she abandoned Cross Creek for re-marriage
and residence in St. Augustine. But at her death she was
buried in an Island Grove cemetery, beneath a marker that
reads simply:

BY HER WRITING,
SHE ENDEARED HERSELF
TO THE PEOPLE OF THE WORLD

PART FIVE:
War, Space, and Mickey Mouse

With the outbreak of World War II, Florida entered her most explosive period. More and more visitors, including Harry S Truman and John F. Kennedy, spent time in the state. Simultaneously, increasing numbers of major enterprises were launched.

Although including the oldest remnants of European colonization in the nation, Florida today is modern in outlook, culture, and opportunities for both visitors and residents.

Colin P. Kelly, Jr., United States Military Academy class of 1937.
[USMA Archives]

33

Colin Kelly Became the First Hero of World War II

"No doubt about it; Colin made a suicide run," General Henry H. ("Hap") Arnold confided to aides. "He makes me proud to be a West Pointer—and makes every American hold his head higher."

Before he issued a formal statement, the chief of the newly established Army Air Force summarized the drama-filled last flight of Madison native Colin P. Kelly, Jr.

"Captain Kelly sighted the Japanese battleship *Haruna*, and recognized her to be heavily armed," he said. "Captain Kelly was at the helm of one of our handful of undamaged B-17s and knew that he would come in range of antiaircraft guns long before he could release his bomb load.

"Yet he flew directly into enemy fire to plant three bombs on his target. My greatest regret is that the brave Florida flier may have gone to his death without knowing that he had accomplished his mission."

When news of Kelly's exploit reached the mainland from Manila, on December 12, 1941, Americans took to the streets. Impromptu parades were staged in honor of the man labeled by headlines as "The Nation's First War Hero."

Part of the jubilation stemmed from a national mood of anger and sorrow after Pearl Harbor. Never before had the United States suffered a blow such as that struck by the Japanese at 7:00 A.M. on Sunday, December 7, 1941.

Tension between the United States and Japan had been increasing for months, yet the attack on Pearl Harbor came as a surprise, crippling the Pacific Fleet. Five battleships were sunk, nine other naval vessels were badly damaged, 200 planes were destroyed, and 2,344 men died on what President Franklin D. Roosevelt labeled as "a day that will live in infamy."

Meanwhile, the Japanese onslaught continued. Nearly simultaneous attacks were made against Malaya, Hong Kong, and the Philippines. Just ten hours after Pearl Harbor, enemy planes hit Clark Field in the Philippines. This time they lost only seven of their planes but left the American Far East Air Corps in shambles. Half of the thirty-five B-17s stationed there were destroyed, along with fifty-six fighter planes and twenty-five other aircraft.

Wartime censorship prevented reporters from getting timely interviews with comrades of Colin P. Kelly, but later some of them confided that the twenty-six-year-old Floridian took a solemn vow within hours after hearing of the attack on Pearl Harbor.

"My crew and I are going to get the attention of Tokyo," he reportedly promised. "It will take only one Flying Fortress to show Hirohito that Americans can't be given a blow below the belly without hitting back—hard."

Piloting a Flying Fortress bomber out of Manila just forty-eight hours after Pearl Harbor, Captain Kelly spotted the Japanese naval task force in Philippine waters. It included the *Haruna,* a 29,330-ton warship. Enemy fire made it impossible to attempt a practice run over the target, so he had to head directly toward her for a single pass, with antiaircraft fire growing heavier as he approached.

Later, General Douglas MacArthur, commander of the U.S. Army Far Eastern Force, issued a one-sentence communiqué: "With great sorrow, I must announce the death of Captain Colin P. Kelly, Jr., who so distinguished himself by scoring three direct hits on the Japanese capital battleship *Haruna,* leaving her in flames and in distress."

Censorship prevented release of details other than a subsequent communiqué that reported the sinking of the *Haruna* on December 9 somewhere north of Luzon.

A Flying Fortress, hit on the ground at Hickam Field in the attack on Pearl Harbor. [NATIONAL ARCHIVES]

In Brooklyn, where she had gone to be with her parents, Kelly's widow met reporters with her arms around her eighteen-month-old son. "My husband was a marvelous officer," she said, "the first West Point graduate to pilot a Flying Fortress. I am very proud of him, and when Colin III gets a little older, he will be very proud, too."

Colin Kelly had been appointed to the U.S. Military Academy in 1933, when he was eighteen. He played football, sang in the cadet choir, and became a crack shot with the pistol. When he graduated, he was commissioned a second lieutenant of infantry. But at a time when the Air Corps was not generally regarded as very important, he requested and got an assignment to that branch.

Less than a week after his death, Florida congressmen began seeking a posthumous Congressional Medal of Honor for Colin Kelly. Five days later, an army air unit in Detroit was named for him. Planes were sent to Madison for a memorial service on December 20, and on December 24 the British American Ambulance Corps began forming a unit to commemorate America's first hero of World War II.

Colin P. Kelly III, United States Military Academy Class of 1963. [USMA Archives].

On December 17 President Franklin D. Roosevelt wrote a directive that began, "To the President of the United States in 1956." Ironically, that chief executive would be the World War II general Dwight D. Eisenhower. Roosevelt's letter requested special consideration of the future president on behalf of Colin P. Kelly III, should he in 1956 wish to become a cadet at the U.S. Military Academy.

"I make this appeal in behalf of this youth as a token of the Nation's appreciation of the heroic services of his father who met death in line of duty at the very outset of the struggle which was thrust upon us by the perfidy of a professed friend," Roosevelt wrote.

Years later, Colin Purdie Kelly III accepted the help offered by President Eisenhower. Kelly graduated from West Point in 1963 and after twenty years in uniform retired as a lieutenant colonel.

The annals of West Point are rich with human interest. But they include no other saga quite like that of the father-son graduates from Florida.

34

America Probes the Universe from Cape Canaveral

Kennedy, Cape: Point of land extending into the Atlantic Ocean about 14 miles northeast of Cocoa and 51 miles east-southeast of Orlando; named for John Fitzgerald Kennedy (1917–1963), the thirty-fifth President of the United States; Brevard County; 28 degrees 27' 30" N., 80 degrees 32' 00" W. Nautical: Cabo de Canareal, Cape Canaveral.
—U.S. Board on Geographic Names, April 2, 1964

The publication of this brief notice completed the legal procedure to change an American place name. For practical purposes, official Washington and the nation at large assumed that the change took place four months earlier, on November 28, 1963.

That evening, President Lyndon B. Johnson broadcast a Thanksgiving message from the White House. Near the end of it, he announced, "Cape Canaveral, site of the United States space facility on the Florida east coast, will henceforth be known as Cape Kennedy."

Jacqueline Kennedy, widely believed to have urged that the change be made, expressed her gratitude to the president and to the nation. "There has been talk of a permanent memorial to my late husband," she said, "but until now, it has only been talk. Cape Kennedy will commemorate his memory during all future generations."

At the same time that he announced the presidential decision to alter the terminology of Florida's map, Johnson said that installations housed there would become the Kennedy Space Center.

Geographer Amerigo Vespucci gave Cape Canaveral its enduring name.

Most—but not all—Americans took the surprise announcement in stride. It was widely known that a proposed national culture center in Washington, D.C., might be named in honor of the assassinated chief executive. Since that project was still in the idea stage, it was generally agreed that renaming the cape was fitting, timely, and permanent.

That point of view did not prevail in Brevard County.

Public reaction was swift, surprisingly strong, and almost entirely negative. Within days, organizers began planning public rallies to protest the presidential mandate. At such gatherings, many people not generally regarded as activists turned up to register their opposition to the change.

"Cabo de Canareal," as the Spanish called it, is the oldest place name in the United States, listeners learned. It is known that it was given that name by the Spanish who came after Ponce De León.

Many authorities agree that it won a permanent place on the map through the influence of Amerigo Vespucci, for whom America is named. He is believed to have modified it to the form that had prevailed for nearly 450 years—Cape Canaveral.

Almost every public rally held in response to President Johnson's surprise announcement ended with a formal resolution. Most such statements praised John F. Kennedy, noted that he was "almost a Floridian through years spent at his father's West Palm Beach home," lamented his untimely death, and demanded a quick reversal of the change in name. "We must not let sentiment of the moment deter us from working to preserve the oldest symbol of European influence in the nation," one set of resolutions ended.

Editors of reference books, either not aware of events in Brevard County or indifferent to them, proceeded to follow the White House mandate. An edition of a popular encyclopedia includes this paragraph:

> In 1513 the explorer Ponce de León claimed the Florida region for Spain. In 1958, *Explorer I*, America's first earth satellite, soared into space from Florida's Cape Canaveral (now Cape Kennedy). The years between these two famous explorers are rich in Florida history.

Accurate when it was printed, that summary failed to take into account the fervor and tenacity of Floridians who were determined to preserve their heritage. Local leaders won friends in high places and exerted mounting pressure. As a result, Cape Kennedy is no longer on the map. Instead, Cape Canaveral is the site of the Kennedy Space Center.

America's annals include no comparable reversal of a decision to commemorate the memory of a chief executive.

It was another occupant of the White House—Harry S Truman—who gave the go-ahead that made Cape Canaveral the jumping-off place for exploring the universe. In October 1949 he established what was then called the Joint Long Range Proving Ground. Few members of the general public realized that devices to be "proved" or tested there were long-range rockets.

Canaveral projects into the Atlantic in such fashion that it provides a starting point for a five-thousand-mile test range over water. Although that was a decisive matter in 1949, the isolation of Brevard County was also a major consideration. For miles around, the area was practically uninhabited by humans.

Military experts cheered on July 24, 1950, when the first launch was made from Cape Canaveral. A modified German V-2 rocket with an attached upper stage achieved an altitude of about ten miles. America entered the space age on that day.

Col. John H. Glenn blasted off from Canaveral on February 20, 1962. The first American to orbit the earth, he made a five-hour trip that prompted Rep. Victor L. Anfuso of Brooklyn to make an enthusiastic proposal. He introduced a resolution in the House of Representatives whose terms required an official change from Cape Canaveral to Cape Glenn. Unlike the later proclamation of Lyndon B. Johnson, Anfuso's resolution was never taken seriously.

Sir Winston Churchill (right) *helped to persuade President Harry S Truman that the United States should build and test long-range rockets.*

Space Shuttle 41—D seemed ready for liftoff in June 1984, but the launch was aborted when the No. 3 engine failed to achieve ignition. [NATIONAL AERONAUTICS AND SPACE ADMINISTRATION]

Fierce loyalty to the time-honored geographical name has made a relatively tiny piece of Florida real estate familiar throughout the world. A listing of famous first achievements made at Cape Canaveral runs to column after column of fine print.

Germans who landed on the Florida beach in 1942 came to cripple the U.S. industrial and military complex. They were foiled by Floridians much like those who balked at the mandate of Lyndon B. Johnson and succeeded in having it rescinded. Ironically, it was other Germans, Wernher von Braun and Kurt Debus, who played key roles in converting the space center at Canaveral from the theoretical to reality.

Thirty years after *Explorer I* put the United States into the space race, Gov. Bob Martinez announced a long-range plan for a state-funded Spaceport at Canaveral. Envisioned as "a port authority for the universe," it promises an economic boom for Titusville and Cocoa Beach.

It is reasonably certain that federal, state, and commercial interests will focus upon this area for decades to come. At the cape first seen by Europeans from the decks of Ponce de León's little vessels, mighty space ships will roar upward toward the limits of the solar system.

35

Brownie Wise Taught the World How to Give a Party

"This is Brownie Wise, calling from Florida. I'd like to speak to the company president, please."

"Hello. This is Earl Tupper. What can I do for you?"

"Mr. Tupper, I hope you can do a lot for me. I'm Brownie Wise, calling from Florida. I'm distributing a lot of Tupperware® brand products, and my shipment is late—for the second time. Can you do something to see that I get deliveries on schedule?"

"Of course I'll do something to correct this situation. But I don't want to stop there. Can you come to Worcester? I'd like to sit down and have a long talk with you."

"Sorry," responded Brownie Wise. "I'd like to meet you, but I can't come. I have twenty dealers who are looking to me to keep their orders filled. If you want to see me, you'll have to come to Miami."

Late in 1949 the inventor of Tupperware products persuaded the Florida divorcee to come to Massachusetts for a conference. He won her over by promising to bring to the company headquarters the half dozen or so other persons who were already distributing and selling Tupperware products on the home party plan.

In Worcester, Earl Tupper soon learned that Brownie Wise had been a distributor of Stanley Home Products, in Dearborn, Michigan, where she had worked as a secretary. For her, the home sale of Stanley products was a sideline, but an important one. A few pieces of houseware made of an unusual new kind of plastic led her to decide to add Tupperware products to her business. Soon she dropped

Stanley Home Products in favor of the faster-moving household bowls and containers of which few people had ever heard.

Much the same thing happened to Stanley distributor Tommy Damigella. He heard of Tupperware products, began buying them from a Boston distributor, and found them to have so much appeal that he gave up all other lines.

At the 1949 conference in Worcester, Massachusetts, Tommy and Brownie exchanged experiences. Four years on the market, Tupperware products had made no significant impact.

Hardware stores and big department stores handling kitchenware were moving only small quantities. Anyone who tried a product made of the new plastic agreed that it had unique qualities, but the public demand was not great enough to induce store owners to push it.

Before the 1949 gathering ended, Earl Tupper was a convert. He decided to give much less attention to wholesale and retail distributors through conventional channels. In fact, he would go for broke by putting the persuasive woman from Miami in charge of sales.

Tupper, who knew little or nothing about organizing a sales program, was a genius of another sort. Trained in chemistry, he visited an oil refinery one day and noticed that waste produced in the refinement of petroleum was made into blocks about the size of a book. No one had the slightest idea of what to do with these black chunks, and they were thrown away.

Questioned by Tupper, a friend explained that the stuff was called polyethylene. "Sure you can have some of it," he said. "Take all you want and see if you can find some use for it."

Major corporations had already experimented with plastics, but the products produced by their research departments had no sales potential. Items made from these plastics had no eye appeal and seemed to break at the slightest contact.

Experimenting in a home laboratory, Earl Tupper

turned polyethylene into a plastic that could be molded by machinery. His initial test pieces did not look as good as the cheapest glass and china, but they did not break when dropped. Encouraged, but a long way from being certain that he had a successful product, Tupper organized a small South Grafton, Massachusetts, company.

That was in 1942, and Tupper was thirty-five years old. It took months to persuade a few retail stores to begin handling the new plastic pieces and, after having been on the market for a decade, the product line was going nowhere until Brownie Wise was put in charge of sales.

She and the dealers she recruited sold only on the home party plan. At her insistence, dealers met annually to share ideas and brainstorm. "You can't beat people over the head and tell them to buy," she insisted from the first. "Plan a party that will give everyone a good time and will permit participants to make a new friend or two. Demonstrate your products, but only after you know them inside and out. Use the soft-sell approach. Show the merits of Tupperware: their range of colors, the unique seal, and their general eye appeal and utility. When you do a good job with this, you won't have to twist any arms. Party participants will buy without any urging."

By 1951 not a store in the nation was permitted to sell Tupperware products. Brownie Wise made the home party plan the sole sales channel. She traveled Florida for hundreds of miles, above and below Miami, looking for a site at which to erect a headquarters building for what she already envisioned as a global enterprise.

"I've found the perfect place," she exulted in a special report to Earl Tupper. "We can build at low cost between Orlando and Kissimmee and be within easy access of good transportation."

Completed in 1954, the new headquarters building was the site of a "Homecoming Jubilee" that was also a national sales meeting—the company's first. Participants flocked to a newly created lake to help dedicate it to Earl Tupper. They swapped party ideas and applauded with

Party planner Brownie Wise with inventor Earl Tupper, dressed for a Jubilee. [TUPPERWARE HOME PARTIES]

enthusiasm when they were told that Tupperware was one of only two major industries in all of central Florida.

In 1951 Brownie Wise agreed to head the newly organized Tupperware Home Parties Division for only one year; she did not want to be out of selling for long. Her first Jubilee in 1954 was so successful that *Life* magazine ran a special story about it, and she agreed to continue helping others to plan parties instead of holding her own.

Earl Tupper's inventive genius produced a line of products with nearly universal appeal. Brownie Wise developed party ideas so imaginative that approximately eighty million people attend them, worldwide, each year.

In 1970 a three-pavilion headquarters building, with a museum, garden, convention center, and park, began to take shape. Tupperware did for Florida's industry what theme parks did for tourism. Today the brand name is familiar throughout the world, simultaneously American and global in much the same sense as McDonald's® and Coca-Cola®.

From the Florida headquarters, perhaps ninety thousand independent direct sellers in the United States receive guidance, along with at least two hundred thousand more who give Tupperware parties in forty-two countries.

Brownie Wise had no idea of the chain reaction she was about to trigger when she placed her first telephone call to Massachusetts. She would be inordinately proud if she were still at Tupperware, but the Florida woman has not sat back and taken it easy while toting up her triumphs. She now consults with clients throughout the United States.

Men have always sold Tupperware, and the changing nature of the work force has made them increasingly important purchasers. Many purchasers—male or female— are not fully aware of what every independent direct seller knows: Tupperware brand products launched the revolution that has brought plastics into every area of life.

A walking tour of the Orlando world headquarters of Tupperware Home Parties is available to visitors. Allow a minimum of forty-five minutes for the lakes, park, garden, and museum. For more information, write to Tupperware Home Parties, P.O. Box 2353, Orlando, FL, 32802; telephone (407) 826-4568.

36

"Somebody's Grabbing Up an Awful Lot of Land"

"What's new these days?" inquired California entrepreneur William J. Canole. Owner of a chain of businesses with investor backing, Canole had stepped into a Stuckey's pecan shop. He had a few minutes to kill while he waited for his private plane to take on fuel.

"Not much," responded a native of Orange County. "Looks like we might get a little shower this afternoon."

He paused reflectively, eyed the stranger up and down, and commented, "Only real news around here is that somebody's grabbing up an awful lot of land. Everybody I know is selling. One fellow just gave an option for a thousand acres."

Canole thanked the Floridian, canceled his planned departure, and returned to his Orlando hotel room. For at least two weeks, maybe three, he had pored over maps and explored the countryside. From California sources, he knew that central Florida was being considered as the possible site of a vast new Disney theme park. If he could pinpoint the site, he and his clients stood to make fortunes.

Central Florida lore insists that Canole and other scouts for big business studied at least half a dozen other sites east of the Rocky Mountains. Dallas was once believed to have been picked by the Disney people, although many signs pointed toward a St. Louis location.

Trying to appear casual while he followed up on the tip dropped at Stuckey's, Bill Canole went back to the courthouse. His informant was right. Unknown purchasers were acquiring thousands of acres of land.

While tourists flock to Disney World by the millions, excellent fishing is available for tourists and Floridians on nearby Lake Tohepakilaga. [KISSIMMEE/ST. CLOUD VISITORS' BUREAU]

Oldtimers in the region, glad to get two hundred dollars an acre for land that was all but worthless even for grazing cattle, joked about the big buy. With the Ford Motor Company's Mustang surging to popularity, many quipped that "Ford is buying up grazing land to fatten Mustangs before putting them up for sale."

At Disneyland in Anaheim, California, executives were tightlipped. They admitted to having plans for a new enterprise that might entail an initial investment of $400 million or more, but they refused to comment where that money might be spent. First they wanted to acquire all the land they needed at rock bottom prices.

At Walt Disney World today, information is still tightly controlled. Telephone calls and letters inquiring about factors that led to the choice of Osceola and Orange counties as the location for the world's biggest theme park brought no reply. Though eager to have photographs in newspapers and magazines, executives refuse permission to use them in books. But it is a different story at the Kissimmee–St. Cloud Convention and Visitors Bureau.

Staff members are not only willing to answer questions and talk freely; they cheerfully volunteer information.

"Lots of folks called both of these places 'cow towns' until very recently," an executive confided. "They were more than half right. Ranchers drove their herds right through the middle of town, down to the depot where animals were loaded for shipment."

Most people who lived in central Florida before the explosion that took place October 1, 1971, concede that the Disney Enterprise scouts knew their business. "They studied tourist flow, climate, population trends, and transportation systems," say natives. "But most of all, they looked for a place where they could get lots and lots of land."

Irlo Bronson, who once owned large acreage now part of Disney World, points out that until it became the site of an entertainment mecca, it really was not worth much. There were orange groves and some good cattle ranches, but, says Bronson, "Lots of that land was consistently too wet or too dry—no good, really, even for use as cattle ranges or game preserves."

Craig Linton, Sr., of Orlando, operated a real estate firm called Florida Ranchlands. By the time he and other realtors finished closing land deals, the Disney people held title to 27,443 acres, a forty-three square mile undeveloped tract in central Florida, more than twice the size of Manhattan Island.

Much earlier Walt Disney had confided that he had a vision of a completely new kind of family entertainment. He wanted lots of room on which to build, and extra holdings for future expansion. A bit wistfully, he more than once confessed, "Here at Disneyland [in California], we have been cramped from the first; it would be wonderful to have the blessing of unlimited size."

Disney agents chose the Osceola–Orange County region in 1964, but kept their plans hidden for more than a year while they acquired the immense acreage they wanted. When they made their announcement, everyone in Osceola County knew that life would never be the same again.

The population of the county was 19,020 in 1960; in three decades it increased nearly five hundred percent. The number of jobs increased tenfold from 4,606. The average annual income moved from $3,368 to just under $20,000.

These local changes are just the side effects from the colossal impact of visitors. A few tourists visited Osceola County as early as the 1940s, but when the Disney location was revealed to an expectant world, the county had just 482 hotel rooms, a figure that has jumped nearly forty-fold.

The addition of EPCOT Center—an Experimental Prototype Community of Tomorrow—brought another huge increase in the number of visitors. Described by many as "a permanent World's Fair," EPCOT has created a ripple effect. So many people go there that traditional World's Fairs such as those in Knoxville and New Orleans no longer have enough drawing power to be financially successful.

Shingle Creek, only minutes away from Disney World, retains much of the tranquility that marked the "pre-Disney era." [KISSIMMEE/ST. CLOUD VISITORS' BUREAU]

In 1971 Economic Research Associates forecast that during the first ten years of Walt Disney World, the theme park would add $6.6 billion to Florida's economy. Tax revenues were estimated to jump by $343 million during that period, and newcomers to the state were expected to spend $70 million on about thirty-seven thousand new residential units.

If that early projection erred, it was on the side of caution. No one has devised a method to measure the impact made by Walt Disney World and EPCOT. With the Disney/MGM Studios theme park added, growing numbers of international visitors make the complex a world center of tourism.

At the same time, other forces have been at work. Satellite facilities and other amusement parks have sprung up throughout the state to reap tourist dollars. Many vacationers find the climate so alluring that they choose to become Floridians.

At the turn of the century, Florida ranked thirty-second among the states in population. During the next fifty years it climbed slowly, to twentieth place. During the twenty years that followed 1950, populaton jumped nearly three hundred percent—from 2,771,305 to 6,789,443. All of this growth took place before the Disney theme park really got started. This "progress" occasionally disgruntles some old-timers. While they like the new prosperity, they have been heard to complain that the state is becoming overcrowded. And the boom shows no signs of diminishing.

The Kissimmee–St. Cloud region is truly a world-class center for family-oriented entertainment. Visitors can drive to either the Atlantic or Gulf coasts in about one hour. They can also include in their itineraries these attractions: Sea World, Busch Gardens, the Kennedy Space Center, Wet 'n Wild, Gatorland Zoo, Tupperware Exhibit and Museum, Alligatorland Safari Zoo, Arabian Nights, Medieval Times Dinner Tournament, Xanadu, Water Mania, and other fun activities.

*   *   *

Juan Ponce de León was pleased to sight what he called
the "land of flowers." But neither the Spanish who followed him, the French and English who fought over it,
the Seminoles and runaways who took refuge in it, nor
the Americans who built winter homes by the seashore in
the early twentieth century, could envision what war,
space, and Mickey Mouse would do to the more desolate
region of central Florida.

*How much time should be budgeted for Disney World,
EPCOT, and the surrounding area? As much as one's
pocketbook and schedule can afford. As an absolute minimum, plan to spend three days and nights when you visit.*

*For Walt Disney World information, address inquiries
to Guest Information, P.O. Box 10,000, Lake Buena Vista,
32830-1000 and allow six to eight weeks for delivery of
material requested. For much faster response and general
information about lodging and entertainment in the area,
contact the Kissimmee–St. Cloud Convention & Visitors
Bureau, P.O. Box 2007, Kissimmee, FL 32742-2000; telephone (407) 845-5000.*

Index